WHERE DID SOCIAL STUDIES GO WRONG?

Edited by James S. Leming, Lucien Ellington
and Kathleen Porter

THOMAS B.
FORDHAM
FOUNDATION

OUTSIDE THE BOX

The Thomas B. Fordham Foundation is a private foundation that supports research, publications, and action projects in elementary and secondary education reform at the national level and in the Dayton, Ohio, area. Further information can be obtained at our website (http://www.edexcellence.net) or by writing us at 1627 K Street NW, Suite 600, Washington, DC 20006. (We can also be emailed through our website.) This report is available in full on the foundation's website, and hard copies can be obtained by calling 1-888-TBF-7474 or emailing fordham@dunst.com. (Single copies are free.) The foundation is neither connected with nor sponsored by Fordham University.

Cover illustration by Darren Gygi. All rights reserved.

Design by Katherine Rybak Torres. Printed by District Creative Printing, Upper Marlboro, Maryland.

August 2003

CONTENTS

FOREWORD

Chester E. Finn, Jr.

For a very long time, the deterioration of social studies in U.S. schools resembled the decline of the Roman Empire: protracted, inexorable, and sad, but not something one could do much about.

Evidence kept accumulating that American kids were emerging from K-12 education—and then, alas, from college—with ridiculously little knowledge or understanding of their country's history, their planet's geography, their government's functioning, or the economy's essential workings.

Evidence also accumulated that, in the field of social studies itself, the lunatics had taken over the asylum. Its leaders were people who had plenty of grand degrees and impressive titles but who possessed no respect for Western civilization; who were inclined to view America's evolution as a problem for humanity rather than mankind's last, best hope; who pooh-poohed history's chronological and factual skeleton as somehow "privileging" elites and white males over the poor and oppressed; who saw the study of geography in terms of despoiling the rain forest rather than locating London or the Mississippi River on a map; who interpreted "civics" as consisting largely of political activism and "service learning" rather than understanding how laws are made and why it is important to live in a society governed by laws; who feared that serious study of economics might give unfair advantage to capitalism (just as excessive attention to democracy might lead impressionable youngsters to judge it a superior way of organizing society); and who, in any case, took for granted that children were better off learning about their neighborhoods and "community helpers" than amazing deeds by heroes and villains in distant times and faraway places.

The social studies problem seemed hopeless. And so I and many others concluded that serious education reformers were well advised to put it on a raft and push it into deep water somewhere in the despoiled rain forest or maroon it on a glacier whose melting is caused by the excessive carbon dioxide emanating from prosperous societies. Put it somewhere far away and hope it will vanish.

PUTTING SOCIAL STUDIES ASIDE

As recently as September 10, 2001, we at the Thomas B. Fordham Foundation were throwing up our hands in frustration—and turning to other challenges. This, despite enormous earlier efforts by us and our antecedent Educational Excellence Network to diagnose and cure the problems of social studies. We had helped with the work of the Bradley Commission on History in the Schools and the launch of the National Council on History Education. We had worked with the National Geographic Society to restart geography as a legitimate school subject. We had served on boards and committees beyond counting. We had evaluated state social studies standards. Back in 1987, Diane Ravitch and I had penned *What Do Our 17-Year-Olds Know?*, which helped expose the breadth of historical ignorance among high school juniors and seniors. We had published books on the decline of the humanities in U.S. schools and what to do about them. We joined with Freedom House and the American Federation of Teachers in 1987 to write and circulate *Education for Democracy: A Statement of Principles, Guidelines for Strengthening the Teaching of Democratic Values*. We had contributed to the State Department publication *What Is Democracy?* (see http://usinfo.state.gov/products/pubs/whatsdem/). And on and on.

We had tried. For the most part, however, we had failed. The forces arrayed on the other side were too powerful, too entrenched in their university posts and their command positions in state education departments. The empire seemed destined to decline until it fell. And so, for the most part, we went on to other issues, to education reform battles where we glimpsed a better chance of making a difference. Not the least of these was a many-faceted effort to bring more choices into education, and not the least of the reasons for that was our conviction that a more open and diverse delivery system would enable educators and parents who cared about history, geography, and civics to find ways of imparting them to their pupils and children. The larger social studies problem, however, seemed hopeless.

Then came the terrorist attacks of September 11 (and their smaller-scale counterparts from Yemen to Nairobi to Riyadh), soon followed by the responses of the "leaders" of social studies. Naturally, the question had immediately arisen of what to teach children about these horrific events. And the despicable answer, from many quarters of the social studies field in particular and the education establishment in general, was teach them to feel good about themselves, to forgive their trespassers, not to blame anyone (lest this lead to feelings of hatred or prejudice), to appreciate diversity, and to consider the likelihood that America was itself responsible for this great evil visited upon it.

Teachers were not urged to explain to their young charges why some bad people abhor freedom and seek to obliterate democracy; why America, because of what it stands for, is abhorrent to those who would enslave minds, subjugate women, and kill those who differ from themselves; why the United States is worth preserving and defending; and how our forebears responded to previous attacks upon their country in particular and freedom in general. Do not teach such things, was the message. They are jingoistic, premodern, doctrinaire, wrong. So signaled the mandarins of social studies.

This was, for us and many other Americans, the last straw, for it signaled that social studies was not some harmless crumbling wreck of a curricular empire, but was instead becoming—with the best of intentions, to be sure—a force within our very own schools that would, unchecked, prevent the rising generation from learning our nation's history and thus erode America's future.

Could we do anything about it? I do not take for granted that we'll succeed. But I couldn't look in the mirror if we didn't try.

GOOD INTENTIONS, STRANGE RESULTS

A second recent event made the effort yet more urgent, though this one was entirely well intended and in other respects praiseworthy. The No Child Left Behind (NCLB) act of 2001 deals with social studies mainly by omitting it from the new nationwide education accountability system. This was not meant, heaven knows, as a hostile act. The authors of NCLB are patriots all and the Bush administration has undertaken commendable efforts to rekindle civic education and deepen historical understanding. Rather, NCLB's authors seem to have concluded that the country would do well to start by getting kids proficient in reading and math (and eventually science), with other valuable (and, compared to social studies, less controversial) subjects left for later. Meanwhile, went the reasoning in Washington, those other subjects could safely be entrusted to states, communities, schools, and educators. NCLB did not aspire to take over the entire curriculum. Perhaps its authors were also deterred by the contentious nature of social studies in particular, the difficulty that some states have had in agreeing on solid academic standards for this fractious field, and the backlash from the uproar a decade ago over national history standards.

In any case, the omission of social studies—and, more importantly, of history, geography, and civics—from NCLB is beginning to have deleterious effects. It's causing some states and schools to downplay these subjects in favor of those for which they'll be held publicly accountable and compared with each other. As the old educator truism puts it, what gets tested is what gets taught. Already we hear reports from the field that history is getting slighted due to the press to get everyone proficient in math and reading. Hard as it is to imagine history getting *less* attention than before in U.S. schools, this is surely not a good thing.

Moreover, as social studies sinks below the watchful eyes of governors, legislators, business leaders, and others who are apt to take a commonsense view of it, it becomes gripped ever more firmly by the field's own leaders, i.e., by ed school professors, textbook authors, state and local social studies supervisors, and their ilk. In other words, those who have brought this field to its present ruinous state—and are major sources of the bad ideas that dominate it—are destined to gain even greater control of it, simply because of the vacuum created when a state's lay leaders focus laser-like upon the challenges directly posed by NCLB: reading, math, and science, to be sure, but also "highly qualified teachers," synchronized testing systems, and other ambitious and difficult undertakings.

To recap: at the very time we most need our citizens and future

citizens to learn what it means to be American and why America is
worth defending, to become more conscious of the world they
inhabit and the conflicts that rock it, to grasp the differences
between democracy and totalitarianism and between free and doctrinaire societies, the part of the school curriculum on which we
must rely for help has turned into a hindrance. It's not getting the
job done. It's wrongheaded. It may even be making matters worse.
Yet we are entrusting it ever more definitively to the hands of those
who brought it to this sorry state. The keys to Rome are being
turned over to the Goths and the Huns.

That's downright upsetting. And while a small private foundation such as this one cannot hope to reverse such mighty forces, we
can at least lend a helping hand to those who are willing to take on
that challenge.

FIGHTING BACK

Accordingly, we made a small grant to a small but plucky band
of social studies "contrarians," as they termed themselves, who
sought to explain what was wrong with this field—their field—and
to suggest how it might be set upon a different course. These brave
souls, led by Lucien Ellington of the University of Tennessee at
Chattanooga and James Leming of Saginaw Valley State
University, yearned to redeem social studies. So we said sure, we'd
provide a little help. Would they be whistling into a gale? Indeed.
Should they nonetheless be encouraged to try? Absolutely. They are
not alone, after all. Having long experience in the field, they are
convinced that most social studies teachers are as concerned as
they are about the state of the field and are hungry for encourage-
ment and direction about how to change it. If any educational good
can emerge from these perilous times, it is a rekindled recognition
by many Americans that the schools have an important role to play
in the preparation of knowledgeable and patriotic citizens.

Messrs. Ellington and Leming and their colleagues have done a
fine job of explaining where and how and why social studies went
awry. I shall not try to summarize their analysis. Allow me, though,
to note that this volume is one of several renewed efforts by the
Thomas B. Fordham Foundation (and the affiliated Thomas B.

Fordham Institute) to open the windows of social studies and allow some fresh breezes to blow through.

Our first effort, as the "anniversary" of 9/11 neared in September 2002, was to publish (on the web only) a collection of short essays entitled *September 11: What Our Children Need to Know*. We are now updating, expanding, and reissuing those essays, both on the web and in hard copy, as a short volume entitled *Terrorists, Despots, and Democracy: What Our Children Need to Know*.

With support from the Lynde and Harry Bradley Foundation, the Fordham Institute is also in the midst of two important studies. One is a fresh analysis of state social studies standards to determine how well they handle U.S. history. The other is a critical review of widely used secondary school textbooks in American and world history.

More will follow. We cannot be confident that our small efforts will have the desired impact on this enormous problem but, fortunately, we are not alone. A number of other organizations—from the National Endowment for the Humanities to the Bill of Rights Institute to the Albert Shanker Institute—are embarked on complementary quests to refurbish this woebegone corner of the American classroom.

What this band of reformers seeks (though their emphases and wording may differ slightly) is to bring the basics back into social studies. In particular, as we noted 16 years ago in *Education for Democracy*, three essential tenets must undergird any decent social studies curriculum for young Americans:

1. Democracy is the worthiest form of human government ever conceived.
2. We cannot take its survival or its spread—or its perfection in practice—for granted.
3. Democracy's survival depends upon our transmitting to each new generation the political vision of liberty and equality before the law that unites us as Americans—and a deep loyalty to the political institutions our Founders put together to fulfill that vision.

To safeguard our nation and its political heritage, Jefferson pre-
scribed education for all citizens "to enable every man to judge for
himself what will secure or endanger his freedom." This is as true
today as ever before. In a world that grows more dangerous, in fact,
it becomes truer and more urgent than ever. In today's political cli-
mate, we are forced to reevaluate what our threats are, who our
allies are, and how we should strive to protect our way of life. It is
essential that we equip our daughters and sons with the tools they
will need to understand the past and prepare for the future. The
point is not to brainwash children. It is to give tomorrow's adults a
proper educational context within which they can understand the
world around them and form their own opinions about it. To that
high end we dedicate this effort.

Washington, DC
August 2003

Passion without Progress:
What's wrong with social studies education?

"That evil is half-cured whose cause we have found."
—St. Francis de Sales

The only possible interpretation of the state of social studies education at the turn of the 21st century is that the field is moribund. The evidence for this dismal assessment is everywhere. Not only is the level of public understanding of our history and cultural traditions alarmingly low, but the willingness of young people to participate in our common political life is also declining. Students rank social studies courses as one of their least liked subjects and social studies textbooks are largely superficial and vapid. Schools of education often appear more interested in producing social studies teachers with politically correct ideologies than producing competent instructors. The federal government recently refused to fund programs to improve social studies education and, nationally, efforts are increasing to replace social studies in the school curriculum with history and the social sciences.

Why is social studies education in such deep trouble? The contributors believe one reason is the dominant belief systems of the social studies education professoriate who train future teachers in colleges and departments of education. These theorists have created and promoted a philosophy of social studies education that has proven to be both educationally ineffective and contrary to the values of most Americans. The perspectives of these social studies theorists rest upon three premises: 1. American society is morally bankrupt; 2. an elite band of university professors, infused with a passion for social justice, knows best how to reform our flawed society; and, 3. classrooms in our nation's public schools are an essential battleground for this societal transformation. The theorists' passion for radical social change and their propensity to use the public schools as a tool to do so, is undoubtedly one reason why social studies is in crisis. It has resulted in a field that eschews substantive content and subordinates a focus on effective practice to educational and political correctness.

The passion of most social studies education professors for radical social change and their belief that the school should be an instrument to achieve that change is, of course, not the only reason social studies is in trouble. Other reasons include: a hostility on the part of many educators at all levels to the kinds of basic knowledge ordinary Americans think important for their children to learn, the neglect of social studies content in many states because of an exclusive focus upon literacy and numeracy to prepare students for standardized tests, and lax social studies teacher certification requirements that result in history and social science teachers who know little subject matter. However, in this book we exclusively focus upon, to use E.D. Hirsch's phrase, the "thought world" of social studies leaders. A thought world that, above all, is infused with the notion that traditional history and social science content and instructional methods should be eradicated in order to better prepare young people to reform our society.

Can this situation be corrected? The current generation of social studies theorists is clearly not up to the task. Social studies education scholarship over the past 20 years has focused on such politicized and often superficial topics as peace studies, the environment, gender equity issues, multiculturalism, and social and economic justice. Although there may be some value in the study of such issues, when they dominate the curriculum, students learn less academic content. Serious issues that classroom teachers should be considering, such as what constitutes appropriate history and social science content and effective subject-matter centered pedagogy, are either transformed by political correctness or largely neglected.

This book is a critical analysis of some of the social studies theorists' most-cherished and loudly trumpeted prescriptions for the schools. As a group, the essays that follow provide readers a cogent understanding of some of the important reasons why today's social studies is a muddled, ineffectual curricular and pedagogical wasteland rather than a coherent, content-based body of important knowledge that is effectively taught and thoroughly learned. In each of our essays, the authors also suggest some solutions for improving history, civic, and social science education in the schools.

Through close association with the social studies establishment and years of reflection upon the dominant belief structures of the field, we have become convinced that social studies is in crisis. The first step in resolving that crisis is to understand its nature. This book is intended to advance that understanding. The contributors to this book are not naïve outsiders or newcomers to the field. With one exception, we are all National Council for the Social Studies members and have held local, state, and national leadership positions in that organization.

• Diane Ravitch is research professor of education at New York University and holds the Brown chair in education policy at the Brookings Institution in Washington, DC, where she also edits the Brookings Papers on Education Policy. In addition, she is a distinguished visiting fellow at the Hoover Institution, where she serves as a member of the Koret Task Force on K-12 education, and a trustee of the Thomas B. Fordham Foundation. Ravitch has written extensively on education and school reform, including her most recent work, *The Language Police*, which has enjoyed enormous critical acclaim. In this volume, Dr. Ravitch presents a brief history of social studies as this 20th century creation veered from the study of history into an amorphous subject based on the whims of those who teach it and devoted at least as much to changing society as to educating children.

• J. Martin Rochester is a distinguished teaching professor at the University of Missouri-St. Louis and author of a recent book on educational reform that has attracted national attention. Professor Rochester critically analyzes civic education and identifies possible causes of the astounding level of political illiteracy that currently exists in the United States. Rochester examines the direct relationship between the progressive's injunction to "teach for active citizenship" and the present state of civic education in U.S. schools. He shows how authors of social studies methods textbooks systematically denigrate the necessity of students actually acquiring substantive knowledge of government and politics.

• Jonathon Burack, a former secondary school history teacher, has for the past 20 years produced secondary school history curriculum materials. Burack chronicles how a global education ideology among contemporary textbook and curriculum writers is undermining quality world history in our nation's schools. He demonstrates the pervasiveness of postmodern cultural relativist epistemology in our nation's schools and argues that hostility to Western culture and its values poses a threat to the development of the next generation's appreciation of American exceptionalism. Students today learn little in social studies classrooms about the leading ideas that Western culture has contributed to the contemporary world.

• University of Tennessee at Chattanooga Asia Program co-director and education professor Lucien Ellington is founding editor of the journal, *Education About Asia*, and has authored three books on Japan. Jana Eaton teaches comparative politics at Unionville (Pa.) high school and has won numerous teaching awards including selection as a *USA Today* All-American Teacher. Ellington and Eaton document how radical separatists dominate multicultural education and advance the notion that the way to teach about other cultures is by accentuating negative aspects of American history and society. They explain the dominance of postmodernism and relativism among university social studies educators who specialize in multicultural education. Ellington and Eaton contend that the ideas promoted by multicultural theorists constitute barriers to students learning accurate content about other cultures and weaken American social cohesion.

• University of Wisconsin-Milwaukee Center for Economic Education director Mark Schug has taught for over 30 years at the middle, high school, and university levels. He is also the author of over 180 articles and books on economics and social studies education. Professor Schug reviews the impressive body of supporting research for teacher-centered instruction (versus student-centered pedagogies) and, through an analysis of prominent social studies methods textbooks, shows this field's denigration of or inattention to this method. He also relates the progressive prejudice against teacher-led instruction to the abysmal results obtained by many colleges of education in training their majors to teach effectively.

• Bruce Frazee is a professor of education at Trinity University, a national Core Knowledge coordinator, and an author of both a college text and an elementary school social studies series. Samuel Ayers, who is affiliated with Lubbock Christian University and the Lubbock Independent School District, was the Texas 1999-2000 Elementary Administrator of the Year. Frazee and Ayers explore the implications of the "expanding environments" curriculum and constructivism on social studies education. They demonstrate how both the nation's most popular elementary social studies curriculum and the hottest current teaching fad in elementary education lack any compelling research base. Although both the expanding horizons curriculum and constructivism contain seductive language and idealistic images, when they are put into practice the result is usually devalued content and children engaged in trivial activities.

• James Leming holds the Carl A. Gerstacker chair in education at Saginaw Valley State University. He is a former member of the board of directors of the National Council for the Social Studies and past president of the Social Science Education Consortium. Leming explores the relationship between two cherished ideals in the social studies worldview: social change and higher order thinking. He shows how the impulse to use the classroom as an agency for social change can only be pursued if it includes antipathy toward tradition and, especially, traditional history. Through an examination of relevant classroom research, Leming demonstrates the lack of an empirical warrant for efforts to teach schoolchildren the types of "higher order thinking" required for policy analysis. The cost of this emphasis is often the neglect of high quality content.

It is critical that all Americans who agree with Thomas Jefferson's argument that the viability of democracy depends, in part, upon the existence of a critical mass of citizens who understand history and public issues read this book. This work contains ample evidence that the beliefs of many social studies education professors work against public civic and historical literacy. The authors of this book are united in opposition to the social studies status quo. Nationally, there is growing evidence that academics, concerned citizens, and political leaders from both parties share our concern that history and social science education in the nation's schools is in dire need of reform. In this year's National Endowment for the Humanities annual Jefferson lecture, Pulitzer Prize-winning presidential historian David McCullough decried the way in which the kind of political correctness exposed in this volume has stripped the American history that today's students study of any message as to why we should appreciate the ideals and sacrifices that have made this country great. He called the emerging national historical amnesia, rooted squarely in vapid politically correct accounts of our history, a threat to liberty: "Something is eating away at our national memory. . . . For a free, self-governing people, something more than a vague familiarity with history is essential if we are to hold on to and sustain our freedom."

Substantial evidence is present in this volume that the reformist progressive impulse of most of the social studies professoriate is simply one more iteration of sentiments that created social studies in the early days of the 19th century. It is the hope of the authors that a critical examination of what we consider to be the largely discredited and educationally dysfunctional notions of the social studies theorists will further stimulate a national debate over the need for quality content in that area of the school curricula we call social studies. Our students and our nation deserve nothing less.

James S. Leming and Lucien Ellington

1

A Brief History
of Social Studies

Diane Ravitch

As one reads these essays, the question of definition reverberates. What is social studies? Or, what are social studies? Is it history with attention to current events? Is it a merger of history, geography, civics, economics, sociology, and all other social sciences? Is it a mishmash of courses such as career education, ethnic studies, gender studies, consumer education, environmental studies, peace education, character education, and drug education? Is it a field that defines its goals in terms of cultivating skills like decision making, interpersonal relations, and critical thinking, as well as the development of "critical" attitudes like global awareness, environmental consciousness, multiculturalism, and gender equity? Over time, it has been all of the above, and the leaders of the field have frequently wrestled with their goals and purposes and self-definition. While some social studies teachers continue to teach traditional history, the leaders of the field tend to see it as a broad umbrella that covers a range of subjects, disciplines, and skills.

Over the past century, the teaching of chronological history was steadily displaced by social studies. And for most of the century, the social studies establishment eagerly sought to reduce the status of chronological history, in the belief that its own variegated field was somehow superior to old-fashioned history. Given the plasticity of its definition, the social studies field has readily redefined its aims to meet whatever the sociopolitical demands of the age were. As a consequence, it is now the case that all history teachers are also social studies teachers, but there are many social studies teachers who do not teach history and who have never studied history.

History, once a core subject of study in every grade beginning in elementary school, lost its pride of place over the years. When social studies was first introduced in the early years of the 20th century, history was recognized as the central study of social studies. By the 1930s, it was considered *primus inter pares*, the first among equals. In the latter decades of the 20th century, many social studies professionals disparaged history with open disdain, suggesting that the study of the past was a useless exercise in obsolescence that attracted antiquarians and hopeless conservatives. (In the late 1980s, a president of the National Council for the Social Studies referred derisively to history as "pastology.")

A century ago, the study of history was considered a modern subject. In the early decades of the 20th century, most high schools in the United States offered a four-year sequence in history that included ancient history, European history, English history, and American history. Most also offered or required a course in civics. Even as the study of history appeared to be firmly anchored in the schools, history textbooks began to improve over the static models of the 19th century, which tended to plod through dull recitations of political events. Historians like Charles Beard, Edward Eggleston, and David Saville Muzzey sought to incorporate political, social, and economic events into their telling of history.

Even the elementary grades offered a rich mix of historical materials, such as biographies of famous men (and sometimes women), history tales, hero stories, myths, legends, and sagas. Teachers for the early grades often took courses to learn about myths, legends, and storytelling, knowing that this was an important feature of their work. Consequently, many—perhaps most—children arrived at the study of Greece and Rome in high school with a well-stocked vocabulary of important figures and classical myths.

Until 1913, history was history and "social studies" was virtually unknown. In that year, a committee of educationists issued a report on the reorganization of the secondary curriculum that placed history into the new field of social studies. This report, eventually published as part of the Cardinal Principles of Secondary Education, was written under the chairmanship of Thomas Jesse Jones, a prominent reformer and social worker who had taught social studies at the Hampton Institute in Virginia to African Americans and American Indians. Jones was one of the first to use the term "social studies." He was a strong believer in useful studies, such as industrial and trade education. He was very much part of the progressive avant garde that believed that academic studies were necessary for college preparation but inappropriate for children who were not college-bound, that is, children of workers, immigrants, and nonwhites. Leading educational theorists, like Jones and David Snedden of Teachers College, viewed education as a form of social work and thought that children should study only those subjects that would provide immediacy and utility in their future lives.

The Jones report on social studies, incorporated into the famous Cardinal Principles report of the National Education Association in 1918, suggested that the goal of social studies was good citizenship and that historical studies that did not contribute to social change had no value. This report, when it appeared and for many years afterwards, was considered the very height of modern, progressive thought. It had a devastating impact on the teaching of history and gave a strong boost to its replacement by social studies. Since it was hard to argue that the study of ancient history, European history, or English history contributed to social change or to improving students' readiness for a vocation, these subjects began to drop out of the curriculum. They were considered too "academic," too removed from students' immediate needs. They made no contribution to social efficiency. The committee in charge of reorganizing the secondary curriculum saw no value in such abstruse goals as stimulating students' imaginations, awakening their curiosity, or developing their intellects.

It was in the spirit of social efficiency that the field of social studies was born. Some educational activists (like Thomas Jesse Jones) thought that the purpose of social studies was to teach youngsters to adapt to (and accept) their proper station in life. Some thought that the goal of social studies was to teach them the facts that were immediately relevant to the institutions of their own society. Some preferred to teach them useful skills that would prepare them for the real world of family life, jobs, health problems, and other issues that they would confront when they left school.

This utilitarian emphasis undercut the teaching of history in the high schools. In the elementary grades, the teaching of history was doomed by the widespread success in the 1920s and 1930s of what was called the activity movement. Educational theorists complained that teaching about heroes and history stories was nothing more than "daydreaming." They wanted the schools to deal "realistically" with the problems of the world. They encouraged the schools to socialize their students by centering their activities on home, family, neighborhood, and community. They said that the schools should teach the present, not the past. One state after another began to eliminate history from the elementary grades and to replace it with expanding environments (home, neighborhood, community). The very idea that students would have fun learning about long-dead kings, queens, pirates, heroes, explorers, and adventurers was dealt with contemptuously by prominent educational reformers as a form of unacceptable escapism from the real problems of society. Socialization, not intellectual enrichment, was the demand of the 1930s and for many decades after in the elementary grades.

During the 1930s, one national report after another insisted that social studies should replace chronological history and that young people should study immediate personal and social problems rather than the distant, irrelevant past. Surely many history teachers continued to cling to their subject. But over time, such teachers became less numerous and, as they retired, others entered as social studies teachers who had been trained to emphasize the immediate needs of youth, current events, and social problems of today rather than the study of the past.

In the rise of social studies and in the diminished status of history in the schools, historians were not innocent bystanders. When it was proposed in the 1920s and 1930s that the study of history should be reserved for college-bound students, snobbish historians were inclined to agree. They too thought that their field should be the preserve of the elite, not a study that was appropriate for the average citizen in a democracy.

For the past 15 or so years, there has been an effort to revive the teaching of history in the schools. Certain states—notably, California, Virginia, Texas, Alabama, and Massachusetts—have created exemplary history standards for their teachers. Many states, however, continue to rank history as but one of a plethora of disciplines encompassed in the all-purpose, hard-to-define social studies. Knowing how controversial any discussion of history is likely to be, many states prefer to avoid any definition of the subject's goals and objectives, finding it far easier to retreat to a fog of generalized and diffuse purposes.

As the present essays show, today's field of social studies is rife with confusion. Its open-ended nature, its very lack of definition, invites capture by ideologues and by those who seek to impose their views in the classroom. This too can happen in the teaching of history, but at least students may encounter contrasting versions of history from different teachers and textbooks, as well as from programs on television and from their independent reading. One hopes that students will emerge from their studies of history, regardless of the views of their teachers and textbooks, with a scaffolding of factual knowledge about the United States and other world civilizations on which they may build in the future.

Ultimately, those of us who reject indoctrination and propaganda in the classroom must recognize that these distortions may occur in any field, be it called social studies or history. Our goal must be to insist that students encounter a variety of views; that their teachers and textbooks recognize the possibility of fallibility and uncertainty; and that students gain a solid body of knowledge as well as the tools and disposition to view that knowledge skeptically and analytically. These are not modest goals, and as the following essays demonstrate, we are far from achieving them.

2

The Training of Idiots
Civics education in America's schools

J. Martin Rochester

*"Together, we will reclaim America's schools, before
ignorance and apathy claim more young lives."*
—President George W. Bush, Inaugural Address, 2001

THE PROBLEM

In Ancient Greece, the word "idiot" referred to an individual who took no interest in public affairs, in the life of the *polis*. America has long been populated by idiots, but their numbers seem to be growing.[1] Increasingly, high school graduates resemble the student who was asked, "What's worse, ignorance or apathy?" and answered, "I don't know and I don't care!" It is debatable which is more alarming, the fact that young people are disengaged from politics or that they are ill informed about it. These conditions would seem interrelated: the less concerned one is about politics, the less likely one is to take the time to become informed; and the less informed one is, the less one's sense of political efficacy and inclination to "get involved." Less is decidedly not more when it comes to what passes today for social studies education in the United States, the field that is entrusted with primary responsibility for developing in American youth their earliest habits of mind about their political system. The purpose of this essay is to explore how the social studies profession may be contributing to the spread of "idiocy" and to suggest what can be done to cultivate a more enlightened and more engaged citizenry.

The problem of civic know-nothingism and do-nothingism is not confined to young people. Regarding the *participation* dimension, as

6

one author notes, "only a small percentage of the American people are actively engaged in the political process. . . . Less than one percent of the population runs for office at any level of government, and only about half of all voting-age Americans bother to go to the polls" (Dye, 2001, p. 138). The "half" applies to presidential elections; off-year elections tend to attract only about a third of the electorate. Presidential voting turnout itself has been in decline in recent decades, from 60 percent in the 1960s to barely 50 percent of late. Even the close Bush-Gore 2000 race managed to attract only 50 percent, while the 1996 Clinton-Dole contest saw 49 percent, the lowest turnout since 1924. (More people watched the "Who Shot J.R.?" episode of *Dallas* and the final episodes of *Cheers*, *MASH*, and *Seinfeld* than voted for the president of the United States.) All told, "the past four decades mark the longest sustained downturn in voter turnout in the nation's history" (Patterson, 2002a).[2] As dismal as these statistics are, they look robust compared to other indicators of political participation, as less than five percent of the population attend political meetings, make campaign contributions, or display buttons and bumper stickers, and roughly 30 percent ever discuss politics (Dye, 2001, p. 138; also see Burns et al., 1995, p. 275; Verba and Nie, 1972; and Milbrath and Goel, 1977).

Joseph Nye and Robert Putnam have commented on the growing cynicism toward politics and government along with the worsening alienation from civil society generally. In an article entitled "In Government We Don't Trust," Nye (1997, p. 99) stated: "American confidence in government has declined. In 1964, three-quarters of the American public said that they trusted the federal government to do the right thing most of the time. In recent years . . . only one-quarter to one-third do" (also see Nye, Zelikow, and King, 1997). Although the rally-around-the-flag impulse after the events of September 11, 2001, gave the President and Congress a momentary boost in public support, that support has eroded as the memory of 9/11 has faded (Stille, 2001). Putnam, in *Bowling Alone* (2000), found that America's "social capital" has been shrinking over the past couple of decades, as reflected in the decline of memberships in what de Tocqueville called "voluntary associations" and in many forms of political participation such as signing petitions, attending town meetings, and working for political parties (also see Uchitelle, 2000). It is beyond the scope of this paper to explain these trends—many factors are likely involved—but the resulting withdrawal from civic space is unmistakable.

If one takes the view that ill-informed political participation is as bad as no participation, then perhaps it is just as well that participation levels are low. On the *knowledge* dimension, the public is widely ignorant of elemental features of the republic (including what it means to be a republic as opposed to a democracy). Fewer than one-third of the American people can name their representatives in Congress or their U.S. senators, and barely half even know that they have two senators (Delli Carpini and Keeter, 1991 and 1996), so that "on even hotly debated congressional issues, few people know where their Congress member stands" (Erikson et al., 1991, p. 295). One observer suggests we are "a nation of nitwits," reflected in a recent Gallup poll showing that "60 percent of Americans are unable to name the President who ordered the nuclear attack on Japan, and 35 percent do not know that the first atomic bomb was dropped on Hiroshima" (Herbert, 1995, p. A15). Public ignorance does not seem time-bound: during the height of the energy crisis of the 1970s, half of Americans thought we were wholly self-sufficient in oil; during the height of Cold War tensions over U.S. relations with the "evil empire" during the 1980s, over half weren't sure whether it was the United States or the Soviet Union that belonged to the NATO alliance; and in the 1990s, with 1 percent of the federal budget going for foreign aid, the public assumed the figure was close to 20 percent.[3] In all, only about 25 percent of Americans constitute what political scientists call "the attentive public" (Burns, 1995, p. 275).

Delli Carpini and Keeter (1996) note that "a consensus has emerged concerning contemporary levels of political knowledge. Studies . . . suggest that knowledge is at best no greater than it was two to four decades ago, and it may have declined on some measures" (p. 116). Based on their own extensive analysis of empirical data between 1940 and 1994, they conclude:

> The good news is that in spite of concerns over the quality of education . . . and the waning of commitment to civic engagement, citizens appear no less informed about politics today than they were a half-century ago. The bad news is that in spite of an unprecedented expansion in public education . . . , citizens appear no more informed about politics (p. 133).

Many apologists for contemporary K-12 education like to argue that, indeed, our schools are no worse than in the past as agents for transmitting civic knowledge. Not only is this hardly a ringing endorsement of our current education system, but it is more an indictment, in that, given the increased access to and expenditure on education since World War II, one would assume civic competency would improve rather than stagnate.

In fact, the current generation of young people may set a new standard for both civic disengagement and civic misinformation. The long-term decline in voter turnout among the general public can be at least partly attributed to the depressing effects of 18-year-olds being given the franchise in 1971—and not exercising it. The percentage of 18- to 24-year-olds voting in presidential elections declined from 50 percent in 1972 to 32 percent in 1996 and 2000.[4] As noted by the American Political Science Association, "the annual CIRP survey of entering college freshmen [compiled by UCLA's Higher Education Research Institute] reports a decrease and record low in interest in politics among the 2000 class," despite the tendency for interest to peak in an election year. "The study found that only 28.1 percent of freshmen were inclined to keep up to date with political affairs, a decline from the record low in 1999 of 28.6 percent and the record high in 1966 of 60.3 percent. The survey also shows a record low (16.4 percent) of freshmen discuss politics frequently, relative to the 16.9 percent in 1999 and a high of 33.6 percent in 1968."[5] It is true that "community service" and "volunteerism" seem to be rising among young people (Plambeck, 2002), but this has not translated into greater involvement in politics.

In terms of misinformation among the young, the statistics are equally alarming.

• On the 1994 National Assessment of Educational Progress (NAEP) American history test, "36 percent of fourth-graders scored below basic; only two percent were advanced. By eighth grade, 39 percent were below basic and only one percent advanced. For seniors, a depressing 57 percent were below basic, with one percent advanced" (*St. Louis Post-Dispatch*, 1995, p. C16). As just one example of factual illiteracy, fewer than one out of three fourth-graders could identify New York as one of the original thirteen colonies, as opposed to Illinois, California, and Texas. Summarizing the results, Lewis Lapham (1995) wrote that the test results "can be read as a coroner's report. . . . [They] returned a finding of mortal ignorance. More than 50 percent of all high school seniors were unaware of the Cold War. Nearly six in 10 were bereft of even a primitive understanding of where America came from" (p. A15).

• Other recent NAEP data: "Less than half the 16,000 high school seniors tested recognized Patrick Henry's defiant challenge, 'Give me liberty or give me death.' Even fewer teenagers . . . knew of the existence of the War of 1812, the Marshall Plan that saved Europe, or Lyndon Johnson's Great Society" (Gross, 1999, pp. 3-4).

• Regarding the very latest NAEP assessment of U.S. history, administered in 2001, Diane Ravitch (2002) writes, "high school seniors registered truly abysmal scores," as 57 percent fell below basic, "an achievement level that denotes only partial mastery of significant historical knowledge and analytical skills. This finding duplicates exactly the awful results of the last U.S. history assessment in 1994."[6]

• David Broder (2000) has observed that "young people are in danger of losing America's civic memory." Writing on July 4, 2000, he commented: "Who was the American general at Yorktown? William Tecumseh Sherman, Ulysses S. Grant, Douglas MacArthur, or George Washington? When that question was asked late last year of 556 randomly chosen seniors at 55 top-rated colleges and universities, one out of three got it right. Stunningly, more of those about to graduate from great liberal arts colleges like Amherst and Williams and Grinnell and world-class universities like Harvard and Duke . . . named Grant . . . rather than Washington. . . . That was not the worst. Barely one out of five (22 percent) could identify the Gettysburg Address as the source of the phrase 'Government of the people, by the people, for the people'" (p. B7).

• A colleague of mine who teaches an introductory politics class at the University of Missouri-St. Louis polled his students at the beginning of the Fall 2002 semester to determine how many could name the current U.S. Secretary of State from among the following choices: John Ashcroft, Dick Cheney, Madeleine Albright, or Colin Powell. That barely half of the class (56 percent) could identify Powell is a sad commentary on student ignorance not only of history but also of current events. (No doubt even fewer could have named Condoleezza Rice, the President's National Security Advisor. How does a student do critical thinking about race in America without being aware that the two cabinet officials largely responsible for foreign policy are African American?)[1]

Perhaps we should not be surprised to find that young people tend to be less informed about politics than their elders, given their shorter life experiences, and less interested in politics, given their lack of substantial property ownership that would enhance their felt stake in the political system. Yet counterbalancing these dampened expectations of civic competency and action are heightened expectations associated with youth's greater immediacy to classroom education as well as youth's greater idealism. In any event, the trends would seem to be moving in the *wrong* direction, with information and interest declining even among young people themselves. As Thomas Patterson (2002a, p. D1) bluntly puts it, "today's young adults are less politically interested and informed than any cohort of young people on record." Insofar as schools are among our major vehicles for performing what political scientists call *political socialization*—"the process by which we learn about politics" (Edwards, 1988, p. 173)—it is hard to escape the conclusion that they are failing in this role. What accounts for this failure to promote civic competence and concern?

THE STATE OF K-12 EDUCATION IN GENERAL

In trying to get a handle on this problem, before focusing on the state of social studies ("civics") education in America, it is helpful to consider the condition of primary and secondary education more generally. Trends in social studies education, after all, may reflect the latest fashions in K-12 at large. There has always been a powerful "pack pedagogy" dynamic at work in K-12. Diane Ravitch (2000) has documented well how, in education circles, the pack has been reading off the same basic script for some time, one written predominantly by "progressives" like John Dewey. She observes that, ever since the education establishment rejected the call, in 1893, by the Committee of Ten (chaired by Harvard president Charles Eliot) for a more rigorous academic paradigm to guide American schooling, there has been a systematic dumbing down of academics and diversion from academics, interrupted periodically by renewed calls for academic excellence (such as in the post-Sputnik era), only to be followed by a renewed commitment to mediocrity.

While these trends are not new, what is different and more troublesome today is that the current school reform movement has a sharper edge than in the past, as *no one* is escaping "the leveler's axe,"[8] not even the best and the brightest. Also worrisome is today's stronger momentum behind progressivism, propelled in part by the Internet and related technological developments, which add wondrous possibilities to the education mission even as they pose potential perils. Some reformers herald technology as a *deus ex machina* for realizing the progressive vision of "every child his or her own Socrates," meaning that instant access to information a fingertip away makes teachers and teaching—at least when it comes to instruction in the basics—superfluous. Teachers, more than ever, are now supposed to "coach" or "facilitate," focusing on "critical thinking" and "higher-order" skills (Rochester, 2002, pp. 175-179).[9] The question is whether this "guide on the side" model is an improvement on what progressives pejoratively call "the sage on the stage" model, or whether progressives have left us with "the Socratic method minus Socrates."

Moreover, there is a bit of a con game going on here: having failed to figure out how to get students to absorb fundamental information, educators have thrown in the towel; but rather than admit such, they now invoke the Internet as a handy rationalization for why specific content knowledge no longer need be taught or tested.

Another double-edged reform sword has been a shift in cultural values. No doubt the decade of the 1960s moved American democracy forward in terms of expanding equality (the rights of minorities, in particular) and individual freedom (freedom of expression, in particular). But we are still living with the excesses of the Woodstock nation, with its volatile fusion of radical egalitarianism and libertarianism (Bork, 1996). In higher education, it has given us postmodernism, which maintains that there is no such thing as factual knowledge, only perceptions based on personal circumstances, all of which deserve equal respect. In K-12 education, it has given us the self-indulgent, nonjudgmental classroom, where rigor and merit are now taboo, for fear of stifling personal creativity or favoring one student over another. E.D. Hirsch (1997a) has aptly dubbed this phenomenon "educational populism."[10]

Our education systems are being turned upside down. While precollegiate educators pretentiously refer to their charges, even preschoolers, as a "community of scholars," college professors often feel surrounded by graduates of South Park and find themselves having to devote more time and energy to remediation, euphemistically called "academic development" (Arenson, 1998). "Constructivism," the modern-day variant of progressivism, theorizes about kids constructing "meaning" when they cannot even construct a simple sentence properly.[11]

The result has been a collapse of standards. Our schools are not wholly to blame for this. However, it could be argued that they have taken the standardless society to new depths. As I tried to explain in recent testimony before the Missouri Senate, commenting on the new "performance standards" that were developed by the state education establishment, which mirrored the standards being developed in other states:

> The dumbing down phenomenon can be seen at work in virtually every school district in the state. Note the widespread emphasis on "self-esteem" and dime-store psychology; "cooperative learning" whereby high achievers are to

be used as free labor to bring up low achievers; the desperate search for a germ of genius in every child, otherwise known as "multiple intelligences theory," which equates slam-dunking a basketball with performing open-heart surgery as a form of brainpower; the nonliterate culture crowding out the literate culture as "visual arts" are now considered part of literacy training, and the latest national English standards now elevate "media-viewing" to a coequal status with reading and writing; the elimination of standards for admission into honors courses, and in many cases the elimination of ability grouping and gifted programs altogether in favor of lowest-common-denominator education; "full inclusion" of behavior-disordered and severely learning disabled students in regular classrooms; reliance on fun-filled, action-packed "activities" as an antidote to "boring" lectures and textbooks, based on the apparent premise that the entire student body suffers from attention deficit disorder; the denigration of substantive knowledge and in its place a growing touchy-feely, mush-and-fluff factor, epitomized by the new Show-Me standard that every student by the time they graduate from high school must be able to "express emotions."[12]

The point is that the problems of social studies and civics education must be understood in the larger context of invented spelling, fuzzy math, experiential and situated learning, the therapeutic classroom and the Oprahization of American education, and other features of the contemporary progressive project. The irony is that, as Hirsch (1997b) has argued, an education paradigm primarily aimed, with the best of intentions, at economic and educational have-nots—the poorest, weakest students—not only undermines the education of high- and middle-achievers but does the greatest disservice to the very clientele that inspired it, since they cannot fall back on parents and outside tutors to provide what the schools do not. Indeed, progressive educators, while claiming to be the agents of democracy who safeguard the masses from "social Darwinists," are the ultimate *elitists*, insofar as their anti-merit, anti-rigor, anti-basics, anti-discipline impulses are at odds with the views held by a vast majority of Americans, particularly inner-city families, as reported in Public Agenda and other surveys (Willis, 1995, p. 5; Stotsky, 1999, p. 201; Sengupta, 1997, p. B8).

The dumbing down of, and diversion from, academics that was just described in Missouri is spreading across the land via pack pedagogy. This trend is epitomized in a recent story in the *Baltimore Sun*, heralding "Howard's Futuristic School," a Howard County, Maryland, high school described as follows:

> "It's a very student-centered school," said [the high school principal]. "To some extent, the older philosophy was you teach content. And now the philosophy is, you teach students." Classrooms are equipped with 27-inch color televisions that connect through phone lines to a "media distribution center" in what used to be called the library. . . . The school store and student government offices are in their own spaces, with storage closets bigger than some elementary school Gifted and Talented Program classrooms. A built-in concession stand is between the gym and the auditorium. "That's something you don't normally have in a school," said [the head of the construction firm]. "But it's something that you need." Concession stands, school stores, state-of-the-art weight rooms, and dance labs—all are necessary these days, school construction experts say (White, 2002, p. B6).

Educational "constructivists" are collaborating with school construction experts to construct schools of the future that give short shrift to academics. "Less is more," as Theodore Sizer's Coalition for Essential Schools[13] trumpets, except, apparently, when it comes to building nonacademic facilities. And "rote memorization" is out, except, apparently, when it comes to self-styled "cutting edge" educators parroting what they have heard in their education schools and professional development training. It is a sad commentary on the K-12 profession that the late Albert Shanker felt a need, toward the end of his life, to write an article entitled "Knowledge Still

Counts" (1996a). Imagine educators needing to be reminded of that maxim. What is perhaps most surprising is that the very school reformers who preach the gospel of "diversity" are themselves often guilty of the most dogmatic and rigid thinking. If "the test of a first-rate intelligence is the ability to hold two opposing ideas in the mind at the same time and still be able to function,"[14] then progressives are flunking. They seem unable to contemplate, in the same breath, rigor and creativity, memorization and understanding, lecturing and active engagement, learning and fun, moral clarity and values clarification, or any other notions that are quite compatible and quite integral to education. Legitimately railing against past excesses—overemphasis on discipline, deference to authority, transmission of factoids, and the like—progressives have *overcorrected* and would now dispose of the baby as well as the bathwater.

THE STATE OF SOCIAL STUDIES EDUCATION IN PARTICULAR

The dominant trends in contemporary K-12 education have predictably impacted social studies, especially civics education. In fact, these trends tend to be most accentuated in social studies, compared to science and other subject areas, for it is in this field, we are told, that democracy demands heterogeneous grouping and cooperative learning, that "service-learning" is essential, that there are mostly opinions rather than facts, that we must be respectful of diverse, multicultural perspectives and learning styles, that we must be sensitive to student emotions and feelings, and that the teacher's role is that of psychologist and problem solver as much as purveyor of knowledge and comprehension—in short, that the non-hierarchical, nonjudgmental, nonacademic classroom prevails. (One might add that it is also in social studies that we typically find most of the staff recruited to coach in the gym and on the athletic field, which suggests where civics education stands in the academic pecking order. Oddly, "coaching" in the sports context means instructing rather than facilitating.)[15]

One need only peruse today's social studies pedagogy textbooks found in our education schools to see the precepts that now guide the teaching of civics. I conducted a small experiment in which I visited the University of Missouri-St. Louis School of Education library, randomly selected five social studies books published in the past decade or so, and performed a content analysis. As a political scientist rather than an educationist, my unfamiliarity with who was or was not a major figure in the field, and who was or was not a "progressive," afforded me an objectivity I might not otherwise have had. I simply wanted to sample the field to see if my impressions of a wayward discipline were accurate. I found that, almost without exception, the pages of these books teemed with progressive nostrums which on the surface sounded as American as apple pie, but upon closer inspection reflected a not-so-hidden agenda grounded in political correctness likely to breed ignorance of the American political system and cynicism toward it.

The first was Shirley Engle and Anna Ochoa's *Education for Democratic Citizenship: Decision Making in the Social Studies* (1988), published by Columbia University's Teachers College Press, which opens with the following passage:

> In this book the social studies are linked incontrovertibly with the democratic ideal. Social studies . . . specializes in the education of an effective democratic citizen. The democratic citizen is not to be understood merely in the classic "good citizenship" sense of who is patriotic, loyal, and obedient to the state; rather, the good citizen is also a critic of the state, one who is able and willing to participate in its improvement (p. 3).

Note the subtle devaluing of positive aspects of American democracy and the stress on "critical" scrutiny of the system. Playing up "critical thinking" and a focus on "controversy" rather than on giving students a basic familiarity with the everyday workings of the political system, the authors add:

> It is our position that the best hope for democracy lies not in indoctrination of shaky truths or in painting over problems that plague us, but rather with the cultivation of citizens who . . . have the facility to make intelligent judg-

ments related to controversial issues in our society. . . . It is of far greater importance to focus on helping young people make intelligent . . . decisions for themselves than it is to tell them what to think. . . . We must stop exhorting students to be "good citizens" according to our own unquestioned view of good and help them instead to ask "good questions" about their own values and those of others. . . . Controversies, rather than fixed knowledge and values, will play a central role in the structure of social studies education (pp. 5-8).[16]

Aside from denigrating the transmission of knowledge and equating it with "indoctrination," note the ostensibly morally neutral posture being promoted, while at the same time setting the groundwork for what is closer to nurturing "America-Worsters" than "America-Firsters," i.e., cultivation of a "let's not trash America, but if we trash anybody, let it be America" attitude.

Note, also, the assumption that uninformed students can make informed judgments. Echoing the anti-intellectualism of constructivist learning theories, the authors state (p. 10) that "dependable and meaningful knowledge seldom comes [from] . . . books or lectures . . . . It must be worked over in the mind and utilized in life situations never before seen and . . . unique to every individual."[17] "Problem-solving" is praised while "mastery of specific bits of information" is put down (p. 27).[18] Ignoring Franklin Delano Roosevelt's dictum that "in a democracy, the government functions with the consent of the whole people, [and] the latter must be guided by the *facts* [italics mine]," Engle and Ochoa (p. 55) insist that "facts learned just to be held in memory" are "next to useless, if not actually harmful."[19] Playing to multiple intelligences and the nonliterate culture, they do praise "art, music, drama" and such, stating (p. 56): "A picture may be more telling than a thousand words. . . . Children may gain greater insight into feudalism from . . . exploring the meaning of a photograph or a clay model of a feudal castle than in reading about feudalism from a history textbook." Were visuals presented as a useful supplement to books, one could hardly object; but they are presented here as coequal, even superior to

reading as an intellectually taxing and rewarding learning medi
um. Missing is any awareness of Benjamin Barber's caution that
"books are a relic of a slowly vanishing culture of the word—democracy's indispensable currency and a faltering bulwark against the
new world of images and pictures flashed across screens at a speed
that thwarts all deliberation. Democracy, like a good book, takes
time" (Barber, 1995, p. 118).

As one reads on, one realizes that the ultimate goal of social
studies education is not only more affective than cognitive in
nature but is calculated to produce not so much skeptics but cynics:

> Citizens of a democracy must be allowed room for doubt,
> even of their own most cherished beliefs. They must
> be . . . able to withstand the socialization process. An
> important responsibility of education in a democracy is
> the *countersocialization* of youth [italics mine]. . . .
> Students are taught how to be skilled critics of the society
> rather than unquestioning citizen-soldiers. . . . [They must
> be liberated] from the dead weight of socialization (Engle
> and Ochoa, 1988, pp. 11-12).

This means that "neither the teacher nor the textbook [should]
serve as a major source of authority" (p. 163). We see here the car-
icaturing of traditional civics education, that to teach is to be a dic-
tator, and to assign textbooks that tell the American story warts
and all, and not just warts, is to misrepresent U.S. history.

Alan Singer's *Social Studies for Secondary Schools* (1997) outdoes
Engle and Ochoa as an exemplar of progressive groupthink. From
the outset, Singer signals his constructivist orientation: "I know
this may sound heretical, but I do not think the specific content
focus of a social studies curriculum should be the main concern" (p.
x). His prescriptions for civics education sound more orthodox than
heretical, as he associates himself with figures who are worshipped
by the progressive education establishment, such as Paulo Friere
and John Dewey. On the student-centered, "democratic" classroom,
he says, "I learned how to organize lessons centered on the interests and concerns of my students, rather than simply on what I

would like to have discussed. . . . [I believe in] the importance of building democratic communities where students are able to express and explore ideas and feelings. . . . I argue that structured experiential learning is the most effective way to teach social studies" (pp. 7-8 and 65). He offers all the standard progressive clichés about direct instruction equaling "chalk and talk" and fostering dreary, dictatorial classrooms.

Deriding attention to facts as belonging to the "Dragnet" (or "Jeopardy") school of pedagogy, Singer goes so far as to state, "I do not believe there are any independent objective criteria for establishing a particular event or person as historically important" (p. 26). By this reading, 1776, the Declaration of Independence, and Thomas Jefferson are no more important than 1969, Woodstock, and Jefferson Airplane. It would seem incontestable that high school graduates should be able to place the U.S. Civil War in the correct half-century and that it is hard to do critical thinking about American democracy if one is clueless about the names of the Founding Fathers whose debates gave us a republican form of government. Today's civic educators consider this "Trivial Pursuit," however, as summed up in the views of Gary Nash, director of the 1994 National History Standards project, who commented that "we want to bury . . . the emphasis on dates, facts, places, events, and one damn thing after another. . . . [We want to] let children out of the prison of facts . . . and make them active learners" (cited in Ravitch, 2000, p. 434).[20] Never mind that, as Delli Carpini and Keeter (1996) note, factual competence is essential to civic competence:

> We understand that effective citizenship requires more than just factual knowledge. . . . Among other things, citizens must also be able to reason, be committed to such fundamental democratic principles as freedom of speech and assembly, share a sense of community, and be willing and able to participate. . . . *Nonetheless, knowledge is a keystone to other civic requisites. In the absence of adequate information neither passion nor reason is likely to lead to decisions that reflect the real interests of the public* [italics mine] (p. 5).

Sean Wilentz of Princeton agrees, noting that educators "pose as courageous progressives dedicated to liberating schoolchildren from the tyranny of rote instruction. . . . But if they have their way, the widely lamented historical illiteracy of today's students will only worsen in the generations to come" (Wilentz, 1998, p. A15).

Citing Alfie Kohn, Peggy McIntosh, and other such luminaries, Singer (pp. 66-67) urges teachers to "take a different approach to motivating students, focusing on the nature of classroom community rather than on particular subject content" and to adopt a "'feminist approach to education' based on an ethic of caring and concern for others." There is the obligatory bow to "cooperative learning," "inclusion," and "multiculturalism" (pp. 126ff and 220ff). To the extent that any exposure to facts is permitted, it must now "include everyone," every conceivable ethnic, gender, or other categorical group (p. 66). The presence in the world of some 1,500 different ethnic groups poses a large time-on-task problem for the 180-day school year.[21] Even the imperative to give equal time to women alongside men can lead to silliness, such as McIntosh's suggestion that Beethoven and Beethoven's mother deserve equal coverage.[22] If our schools in the past were excessively exclusionist and dominated by a Western canon focused on "DWEMS" (dead white European males), we now have what could be called the "Pachelbel canon" approach to history that threatens to trivialize the past (the latter being the theme music from the movie "Ordinary People"). For better or worse, DWEMS dominated much of the political history of the world, certainly the history of the United States. If one really believes in situational learning, then one should heed Edwin Yoder's advice:

[Young people] need to learn first about our own [U.S.] traditions, and those from which they derive. You can't understand the ideas in the Declaration of Independence without knowing a bit about John Locke's treatise on government. Locke leads back into the English revolution of 1688. And that may lead back to the Magna Carta. . . . We should learn who we are before we venture to learn who we aren't (Yoder, 1996, p. B7).

Given the fact that the standards for what constitutes historical accuracy and mastery are so low, we should not be surprised that Singer (p. 64) believes students, by the time they reach high school if not sooner, are ready to "become historians and social scientists." In keeping with the mantra of "active learning," students must not be content to learn history, but must *do* history! Peter Martorella, in *Teaching Social Studies in Middle and Secondary Schools* (2001), agrees. Like Singer, Martorella proudly bares his progressive, constructivist credentials at the start, acknowledging his debt to Dewey, Engle, and others, and his commitment to "countersocialization" (pp. 24 and 28). He states that

> . . . the basic purpose of the social studies curriculum across the grades is to develop reflective, competent, and concerned citizens. . . . Reflective individuals are critical thinkers who make decisions and solve problems. . . . Competent citizens possess a repertoire of skills to aid them in decision making and problem solving. Concerned citizens investigate their social world, identify issues they identify as significant, exercise their rights, and carry out their responsibilities as members of a social community. . . . [Social studies should be viewed as] a matter of the head, the hand, and the heart. The head represents reflection, the hand denotes competencies, and the heart symbolizes concern (p. 29).

Note that not only is the mind considered no more important than the hand, but the mind does not even include knowledge, as one is expected to reflect upon something one does not possess. We have come a long way since Jeremiah Day and James Kingsley, in their 1830 *Reports on the Course of Instruction in Yale College*, remarked about education that "the two great points to be gained . . . are the discipline and furniture of the mind—expanding its powers, and storing it with knowledge."[23] Today there is no discipline, and the room is barren of furniture.

However, there are plenty of "intelligences," as Martorella (p. 383) endorses multiple intelligences (MI) theory, urging that students "should engage in activities that draw on both hemispheres of the brain."[24] I am reminded of an advertisement that read as follows: "*Adventure Tales of America: An Illustrated History of the United States, 1492-1877* fully integrates recent learning research in a U.S. history textbook. . . . Through its multicultural emphasis, strong role models, and dramatic style, students experience U.S. history as a personal adventure. The key to this textbook is its left brain/right brain format. . . . It presents U.S. history to both sides of the brain simultaneously through: words and analysis for the logical, sequential left brain, and pictures, humor, emotion, and drama for the creative, global right brain."[25] We have here not only the possibility of rewriting American history but also refeeling, reenacting, and redrawing it.

Jack Zevin's *Social Studies for the Twenty-First Century* (2000) offers a more balanced treatment that blends traditionalism with progressivism, but is still relatively heavy on the "fun" part of the equation. He reveals his priorities in a "personal prologue":

> Part of the reason social studies is disliked by so many secondary students is that it holds out the promise of . . . vibrant discussion and debate . . . [but] didactic or knowledge aims nearly always triumph over reflective reasoning and ethical arguments. The "sexy stuff" . . . caves in to the "laundry list" of purportedly vital knowledge of dates, names, places, and books. . . . I remember very vividly how bored my urban, inner-city classes were with the facts they had to know and how lively they would become when they . . . [were given] a chance to "spout off" (p. xiv).

"Spouting off" used to be called "bull sessions." Now it is considered "education." Among the suggestions he offers for promoting such modes of analysis is a "drama-building strategy," that is, a pedagogy that "examines the emotional impact of a story, person, event, or document and often yields a sense of catharsis and involvement for the learner" (p. 107). As for the "sexy stuff," he says "students generally enjoy a good story line, especially if it involves adventure, sexual innuendo, or tension among characters"

(p. 107).[26] In other words, history as soap opera. He adds that "music is a lovely change of pace from the words that seem to dominate social studies" (p. 368).

Zevin struggles, as do most social studies educators, with how, on the one hand, to teach "citizenship education" as *American* citizenship while, on the other hand, not promoting too narrow and nationalistic a worldview. The way he and most of his colleagues resolve this issue is to promote global citizenship over U.S. citizenship. One problem is that the concept of global citizenship assumes there is a universal set of values accepted worldwide, which of course is nonsense, given the fact that a majority of states are "not free" or only "partly free" and are habitual human rights violators (Freedom House, 2002). Another problem is that the American experience is now to be treated as just another story, to be "integrated" into the larger human story.

However, Arthur Schlesinger (1992) has argued persuasively that the very intellectuals who preach "integration" and "inclusion" are in effect promoting the "balkanization" of America by legitimizing divisive, group identity politics over the "melting pot" metaphor.[27] Jeffrey Mirel (2002, p. 50) notes that, whereas at one time the "Common School ideal" was to teach "the common American culture" and "civic values" grounded in the Declaration of Independence and the Constitution and to "awaken [in immigrant children especially] a reverence for . . . those things in our national life which we as a people hold to be of abiding worth," now everything is up for debate, including whether it is appropriate for educators to focus on "national" life.

Moreover, Zevin shares the dominant view among social studies gurus that not only has the teaching of American history over the years been too exclusionary, but it has also been too "sanitized" and "self congratulatory" (pp. 255 and 265). While hc (p. 279; also see p. 398) recognizes that "all civics . . . courses face a built-in dilemma—how to balance socialization with criticism," he fails to acknowledge the extent to which "countersocialization" has prevailed. Diane Ravitch (2002, p. 9) has noted "a strong tone of cultural resentment [that] pervades" many social studies textbooks today.[28] To paraphrase Gary Nash, teaching about the

American political system has become the chronicling of one damn victim after another.

One need only witness the various prescriptions of "what to teach about 9/11" offered by the National Education Association and other elements of the K-12 establishment on the first anniversary of that horrific day to realize the latter's reluctance to associate themselves with the patriotism that gripped much of the rest of the country. The suggested "lesson plans" were a textbook example of the trends toward not only the nonjudgmental classroom but also the therapeutic, fact-free classroom.[29] Astonishingly, the website of the National Council of the Social Studies in September 2002 stressed the teaching of tolerance as an antidote to "the anti-democratic" forces at work in the United States represented by the Bush administration, and listed as its *first* recommended lesson plan a look at the internment of Japanese-Americans that followed Pearl Harbor.[30] This was consistent with the advice given by a keynote speaker at the annual meeting of the National Council for Social Studies just two months after 9/11, who "warned against patriotic displays like the singing of 'God Bless America'" (Hymowitz, 2002).

Again, to the extent criticism is permitted, it tends to be criticism of the United States (e.g., the kind of "why do they hate us, what have we done wrong?" self-flagellation that followed 9/11). Given the at best neutral, at worst negative, portrait painted of American democracy, we should perhaps not be surprised at young people's civic lethargy. As a solution to this lethargy, Zevin, like many other educators, stresses the importance of less seat time in class and more "community experience, volunteer work, and precinct-level door-to-door campaigning," as well as other forms of "activism" (pp. 264 and 274). Of course, if schools were not so busy producing cynics and instead engaged children in deep, profound, substantive discussion of the promise and problems of American democracy, perhaps they would not have to resort to coerced volunteerism and other academic diversions (like conflict resolution).

In *Teaching and Learning Secondary Social Studies* (1991), the final book I examined, Arthur Ellis, Jeffrey Fouts, and Allen Glenn come closest to presenting a balanced view of civics education, one that respects a "knowledge-centered" approach (focused on subject matter content) alongside a "society-centered" approach (focused on problem solving) and a "learner-centered" approach (focused on activities). Alas, however, even these authors cannot bring themselves to rate the "knowledge-centered" approach first among equals, as they associate it with "negative attitudes" students have toward social studies, only grudgingly concede the need for testing "low level" information, and conclude that "the truth is that there is no perfect center of the social studies curriculum" (pp. 67, 134, and 19). Here, too, they cannot resist repeating the pabulum found in the other books: "To effectively incorporate the experiences, voices, struggles, and triumphs of marginalized groups in the social studies, the curriculum must be reconceptualized and transformed .... The development of a transformative social studies curriculum presents a major challenge . . . [requiring] new ways of thinking about the United States and the world" (p. 277).[31]

The bigger challenge facing American education would seem to remain one of training students who are not idiots when it comes to civic competence and concern. It is fine to "think globally," but can graduates of America's schools "act locally," in an informed, positive manner, when it comes to their *own nation*? Walter Parker (2003), a leading theorist of citizenship education, raised this very question in a symposium at the 2002 annual meeting of the National Council for the Social Studies, entitled "From Idiocy to Citizenship." The answer seems to continue to elude today's social studies trendsetters.

THE SOLUTION

We need to improve *both* civic information *and* civic interest on the part of our youth. If the earlier paradigm of K-12 civics education suffered from a sanitized, exclusionist bias, a tendency toward information overkill, or other such flaws, we now have overcorrected in the other direction. We still do not have the balance right. What do we need to do?

• First, we need to reaffirm the importance of students studying American history—*their* history—in its own right, and not merely as part of some "integrated" world history. Moreover, we need to provide a more accurate rendering of American history. While acknowledging the contributions of the Grimke sisters and of "ordinary" people and people of color, we also need to give proper space to Washington, Jefferson, and the true heroes of the American story.[32]

• Second, we need not be bashful about the extraordinary achievements of the American political system, which has, after all, produced the largest, most successful, most prosperous experiment in mass democracy in the million years humanity has been on the planet.[33] While acknowledging a racist, sexist past that still lingers to an extent, we should read aloud to our students the words of Vaclav Havel, the Czech poet who helped lead his country out of communist dictatorship in the 1980s. Speaking before the U.S. Congress after the fall of the Berlin Wall, he said: "As long as people are people, democracy, in the full sense of the word, will always be no more than an ideal. In this sense, you, too, are merely approaching democracy. But you have one great advantage: you have been approaching democracy uninterruptedly for more than 200 years."[34]

• Third, we need to stress the importance of students starting with a common base of factual information about the American historical and contemporary experience. While promoting higher order thinking skills, we must acknowledge that this is not only compatible with memorizing names, dates, statistics, etc., but presupposes the latter. Precise recall is less important than developing a solid "ballpark" sense of history and the present, one that is stored in the brain rather than requiring constant "on-line access." At the same time, we should experiment with pedagogical strategies that may more successfully enable teachers to produce such factual literacy.[35] Before students can be expected to save the planet, they need to have at least a rough picture of what they are up against, of what reality looks like. The "Position Statement" on "Creating Effective Citizens," published by the National Council for the Social Studies in 2001, hints at the importance of insuring each student "has knowledge of our nation's founding documents, civic institutions, and political processes," but does not go far enough—relegating this to the middle rank of 10 goals.[36]

• Fourth, we need to cultivate teachers who are not only passionate about kids but about their subject matter. Such passion, as Shanker (1996b) noted, tends to be correlated with deep subject matter expertise.[37] We need teachers who not only have read books on teaching about slavery and the Holocaust but also have read books *on* slavery and the Holocaust. Process is no substitute for content. Teaching about politics is more likely to come alive with a serious, captivating lecturer than with fun and games. There is a need to develop stronger links between the pedagogical experts in schools of education and the content experts in arts and sciences.[38]

• Fifth, we need to engage students in the right ways. While there is a place for service-learning, participation inside or outside the classroom must be meaningful if it is to translate later into participation at the polling booth and elsewhere in the political arena. "Kids Voting," a nationwide program that utilizes the school setting to get children to accompany their parents to the polls on election day, has proven successful as a civic initiation rite for many young people.[39] More such efforts must be tried.

• Finally, we need to create fewer doubters and cynics. Politics in America works, however imperfectly. True, education is mostly about getting students to cope with ambiguity. Yet ambiguity does not mean the absence of truth, only its complexity. Instead of promoting intellectual and moral relativism—nihilism—we should give children the strong grounding in knowledge and values that will hopefully result in a greater sense of political efficacy.

Only then will the *polis* have a chance of surviving and flourishing.

NOTES

1. The lament about the political ignorance and apathy of the American people is not new. Among the writings that have noted the lack of public affairs information and involvement long demonstrated by the average U.S. citizen, and particularly younger citizens, over the years are Remmers (1957), Mathews (1985), and Cronkite (1983). Wineburg (2001, pp. vii-viii) does an especially effective job in chronicling the periodic hand-wringing over the absence of historical knowledge possessed by high school graduates, beginning with J. Carleton Bell and David McCollum's 1917 piece in the *Journal of Educational Psychology*. My argument here, however, is not that this is an unprecedented problem, only that what evidence exists suggests that it seems to be worsening. See evidence below.

2. In each presidential election between 1860 and 1900, at least 70 percent of the electorate voted, with over 80 percent voting in 1860 and 1876, although some analysts argue that voter fraud inflated these numbers. Voting turnout trends are reported in Patterson (2002b); Wilson and Dilulio (1998, pp. 149-150); and Dye (2001, p. 143).

3. On energy, see "Only About Half of Public Knows U.S. Has To Import Oil, Gallup Survey Shows," *New York Times*, June 2, 1977. On NATO, see the 1981 Washington Post-ABC News poll, reported in *Interdependent*, 7 (November 1981), p. 1; also the 1983 CBS-New York Times poll cited in *National Journal* (August 8, 1983), p. 1658. On foreign aid, see Barbara Crossette, "U.S. Foreign Aid Budget: Quick, How Much? Wrong," *New York Times*, February 27, 1995.

4. Data are from U.S. Census Bureau, accessed on the Internet at www.census.gov/population/socdemo/voting/tabA-1.

5. "Election Year Interest in Politics Marks Record Low," accessed on the Internet at wysiwyg://4/http://www.apsanet.org/teach/freshmen.cfm.

6. Diane Ravitch, "Statement on NAEP 2001 U.S. History Report Card," released on May 9, 2002, accessed on the Internet at http://nagb.org/naep/history_ravitch.html. Also, see "Study: History Still A Mystery to Many Students," *Washington Post*, May

10, 2002, which reports "six in ten seniors lack basic knowledge."

7. One commentator argues that American students do well on tests of "civic knowledge" relative to foreign students. Examining the results of a 1999 test administered to over 2,000 ninth-graders in 28 countries, Carole Hahn (2001b, p. 456) reports that "on the overall test . . . U.S. students performed above the mean. Moreover, U.S. students did exceptionally well on [some items measuring higher order skills]. . . . On the subscale measuring knowledge of content, U.S. students did not differ from the international average." Before proclaiming this as "good news," however, it may be instructive to note that a recent *Guardian* newspaper poll in Britain found that "young 18- to 24-year-old British adults are measurably 'dumber' than older age groups. British youth emerge consistently as knowing less . . . than older people about many of the main events and personalities of British history and culture. Fewer than a third of them can name Winston Churchill, Britain's wartime hero, as a prime minister who served before 1945" (Ezard, 2000).

8. The reference here is to how the Bronx High School of Science, Stuyvesant High School, and Brooklyn Technical High School in New York City have struggled to remain elite schools with difficult admissions tests and strong academic programs, resisting efforts to make them more "egalitarian." Mac Donald (1999) notes they "are everything the public school system has mistakenly tried to eradicate."

9. On the need for "student-centered" classrooms where teachers should be "in more of a coaching role . . . —a 'guide on the side,' helping students find answers online, rather than a 'sage on the stage,'" see Darling-Hammond (2001, p. 61). She was head of the National Commission on Teaching and America's Future.

10. For a discussion of the attack on knowledge, see Hirsch (1996). He was labeled an elitist when his *Cultural Literacy* (1987) made the case for a common core of basic factual knowledge all American students should be exposed to.

11. On constructivism, see Evers (1998) and Phillips (1995).

12. Testimony before the Missouri Senate, Jefferson City, on January 16, 1996. These criticisms have been sounded nationwide. See Ravitch (2000), Hirsch (1996), Gross (1999), and Sykes (1995).

13. The Coalition for Essential Schools preaches John Dewey's gospel of "less is more" (i.e., study a few topics in depth rather than maximizing content), work in cooperative groups while minimizing grades and competition, emphasize critical thinking rather than accumulation of knowledge, and coach rather than teach. See Sizer (1984).

14. The quote is from F. Scott Fitzgerald's *The Great Gatsby*.

15. In my own child's school district of Clayton, Missouri, I could see the lack of respect accorded social studies as a serious academic discipline when, in the middle school, two science teachers formed an "expeditionary learning" team that took responsibility for teaching not only science but also social studies. It is hard to imagine the shoe on the other foot, that is, two social studies teachers being entrusted with teaching their students about molecular biology and other scientific topics.

16. On the importance of generating controversy—heat more than light—see Hahn (2001a).

17. The authors add, on p. 79, "learners must see a clear connection between subject matter and their lives. This emphasis suggests that the topics and issues studied need to be defined in terms of the interests and concerns of the students."

18. On the importance of problem solving, also see pp. 40-41. On the put-down of direct instruction, see pp. 108-109.

19. The authors state on p. 62, "education that emphasizes isolated facts is not only useless, it is, above all things, harmful."

20. For further discussion of the controversies surrounding the national history standards, see Ravitch (2000, pp. 433-437) and Rochester (2002, pp. 159-164).

21. Rosenau (1990, p. 406) counts at least 1,500 distinct ethnic groups. Another study (Russett and Starr, 1996, p. 48) counts as many as 5,000 such communities.

22. See Farney (1994). One hears similar notions that, for example, the abolitionist Grimke sisters deserve the same attention in history class as some more famous male figures, or that Fannie Lou Hamer, a 1960s Mississippi civil rights activist, rates coverage no less than Martin Luther King.

23. I am indebted to Robert Bliss, Dean of the Honors College

at UM-St. Louis, for calling my attention to this quote, which appears in the Honors College Handbook.

24. MI theory is mainly the brainchild of Howard Gardner. See Gardner (1983).

25. I received this in the mail from a colleague. A related ad, featuring "Adventure Tales of the Constitution of the US," appeared in *Social Education*, 66 (April 2002), p. 140.

26. In fairness, on p. 337, Zevin acknowledges that "the educational and entertainment functions of a lesson must be balanced."

27. One is reminded of Al Gore's misspoken words during the 2000 presidential election, when on the campaign trail he mangled the national motto as "out of one, many." For an anti-assimilationist message that denigrates the concept of the American "nation," see Cogan et al. (2000).

28. Ravitch argues that the desire by textbook companies to avoid offending any ethnic or other minority has resulted in far more "sanitized" history than that criticized by progressives. Hahn (2001b) adopts a typically politically correct view toward these issues, obsessing over male vs. female, white vs. black and Hispanic, and other such group differences. A classic example of the tendency of K-12 leaders to fuel identity politics and malign American democracy was a workshop given in August 2002 in Missouri's upscale Parkway school district, which dealt with "oppression" by whites, males, and the rich. I was left wondering if next year's workshop would be on white, male, rich "occupation." On this theme, see Murray Levin's *Teach Me! Kids Will Learn When Oppression Is the Lesson,* which received a glowing review in *Social Education*, 65 (March 2001), pp. 127-128.

29. For example, see "Teaching About Tragedy," a special issue of *Social Education*, 65 (October 2001), which was essentially morally neutral, and Kohn (2001/2002), which was unabashedly critical of the United States. Kohn himself is hardly a fringe character but is arguably mainstream, having appeared recently as a keynote speaker at the NCTE and NASS annual meetings. Criticisms of the NEA and the educational establishment can be found in Will (2002) and Sorokin (2002). The NEA's prescriptions were in marked contrast to Thomas Friedman, "9/11 Lesson Plan," *New*

York Times, September 4, 2002, and the remarks by Harvard President Lawrence Summers, delivered on September 11, 2002, both of which called for "moral clarity" against "evil."

30. "Teachable Moments," the homepage of the National Council of Social Studies, accessed on September 24, 2002, at www.socialstudies.org/resources/moments/. The "anti-democratic" reference was in a statement by NCSS President Adrian Davis. These themes were struck in her presidential address, published in *Social Education*, 66 (January/February 2002), pp. 6-7 and 72.

31. The words are those of James Banks, quoted approvingly by the authors toward the end of their book. The authors also devote considerable space to Piaget, Gardner, and other well-known progressive thinkers and to discussions of active and cooperative learning and diverse learning/teaching styles.

32. Many critics of the National History Standards project noted the sparse mention of some of the major figures of American history. For example, Lynne Cheney (1994) noted that "Harriet Tubman . . . is mentioned six times. Two white males who were contemporaries of Tubman, Ulysses S. Grant and Robert E. Lee, get one and zero mentions, respectively. Alexander Graham Bell, Thomas Edison [and other such names] . . . make no appearance at all."

33. Historian Walter McDougall, commenting on the National History Standards, observed: "If the 'Founding Fathers' (the term has been banished) invoked human rights, it was to deny them to others. If businessmen built the most prosperous nation in history, it was to rape the environment and keep workers in misery." Cited in Ravitch (2000, p. 436).

34. Vaclav Havel, address before a joint session of both houses of the U.S. Congress, February 21, 1990.

35. Wineburg (2001) offers some useful insights here. Also, see Sansone (1999), although the author still tends to elevate process over content.

36. The statement appeared in *Social Education*, 65 (September 2001), p. 319.

37. Also see Baines and Stanley (2000).

38. A good model is the NSF Learning Package Project I direct-

ed in the 1970s, which brought renowned scholars (e.g., Kenneth Boulding, former president of the American Economics Association) together with cutting-edge pedagogical thinkers (e.g., William Coplin, who headed the Consortium for International Studies Education). Another example is a course currently being offered to current and future K-12 teachers on my campus at the University of Missouri-St. Louis, that is being team-taught by faculty from political science and the school of education along with a high school instructor.

39. "First Vote" is a program being initiated in Philadelphia. E.J. Dionne (2002, p. A23) suggests, "What about election night dances or concerts? If you voted, you get in." This may be wrongheaded incentivizing, but there may be other imaginative ways of encouraging student involvement.

REFERENCES

Arenson, K. (1998, May 31) Classes are full at catch-up U. *New York Times*, section 4, p. 4.

Baines, L. A. and G. Stanley (2000, December) We want to see the teacher: constructivism and the rage against expertise. *Phi Delta Kappan*, 82, 327-330.

Barber, B. (1995) *Jihad Vs. McWorld*. New York: Times Books.

Bork, R. (1996) *Slouching towards Gomorrah: Modern liberalism and the American decline*. New York: Regan.

Broder, D. (2000, July 4) Young people are in danger of losing their civic memory. *St. Louis Post-Dispatch*, p. B7.

Burns, J.M., J.W. Peltason, T. E. Cronin, and D.B. Magleby (1995) *Government by the people* (16th ed.). Englewood Cliffs, NJ: Prentice-Hall.

Cheney, L. (1994, October 20) The end of history. *Wall Street Journal*, p. A22.

Cogan, J. et al. (2000, January/February) Citizenship and the democratic imagination in a global/local context. *Social Education*,

64, 48-52.

Cronkite, W. (1983, February 19) TV audience overexposed, under informed. *New Orleans Times-Picayune*.

Darling-Hammond, L. (2001, October 29) Commentary in *Newsweek*, 61.

Delli Carpini, M.X. and S. Keeter (1991) The U.S. public's knowledge of politics. *Public Opinion Quarterly*, 55, 583-612.

Delli Carpini, M.X. and S. Keeter (1996) *What Americans know about politics and why it matters*. New Haven: Yale University Press.

Dionne, E.J. (2002, August 2) What young voters want. *Washington Post*, p. A23.

Dye, T. R. (2001) *Politics in America* (4th ed.) Upper Saddle River, NJ: Prentice-Hall.

Edwards, D.V. (1988) *The American political experience* (4th ed.). Englewood Cliffs, NJ: Prentice-Hall.

Ellis, A.K., J.T. Fouts, and A.D. Glenn (1991) *Teaching and learning secondary social studies*. New York: Harper Collins.

Engle, S.H. and A.S. Ochoa (1988) *Education for democratic citizenship: decision making in the social studies*. New York: Teachers College Press.

Erikson, R.S., N.R. Luttbeg, and K.L. Tedin (1991) *American public opinion* (4th ed.). New York: Macmillan.

Evers, W.M. (1998) From progressive education to discovery learning. In W.M. Evers (Ed), *What's gone wrong in America's classrooms* (pp. 1-21). Stanford: Hoover Institution Press.

Ezard, J. (2000, October 28) Poll finds young Brits 'dumber' than oldsters. *The Guardian*.

Farney, D. (1994, June 4) For Peggy McIntosh, 'Excellence' can be a dangerous concept. *Wall Street Journal*, p. A1.

Freedom House (2002) *Freedom in the world 2001-2002*. New Brunswick, NJ: Transaction Publishers.

Gardner, H. (1983) *Frames of mind: The theory of multiple intelligences*. New York: Basic Books.

Gross, M. (1999) *A conspiracy of ignorance*. New York: Harper Collins.

Hahn, C. (2001a, November/December) What can be done to encourage civic engagement in youth? *Social Education*, 65, 108-110.

Hahn, C. (2001b, November/December) Student views of democracy: The good news and bad news. *Social Education*, 65, 456-460.

Herbert, B. (1995, March 1) A nation of nitwits. *New York Times*, p. A15.

Hirsch, E.D., Jr. (1987) *Cultural literacy*. Boston: Houghton Mifflin.

Hirsch, E.D., Jr. (1996) *The schools we need and why we don't have them*. New York: Doubleday.

Hirsch, E.D., Jr. (1997a, Winter/Spring) An address to the California State Board of Education. *Common Knowledge*, 4-8.

Hirsch, E.D., Jr. (1997b, March/April) Why traditional education is progressive. *The American Enterprise*, 42-45.

Hymowitz, Kay S. (2002, May 6) Anti-Social studies. *Weekly Standard*, 007.

Kohn A. (2001/2002, Winter) Teaching about September 11. *Rethinking Schools*. http://www.rethinkingschools.org/special_reports/sept11/16_02/kohn162.shtml

Lapham, L. (1995, December 2) Ignorance passes the point of no return. *New York Times*, p. A15.

Mac Donald, H. (1999, Spring) How Gotham's elite high schools escaped the leveler's axe. *City Journal*, pp. 68-79.

Martorella, P. (2001) *Teaching social studies in middle and secondary school*, (3rd ed.). Englewood Cliffs, NJ: Prentice-Hall.

Mathews, D. (1985, November/December) Civic intelligence. *Social Education*, 678-681.

Milbrath, L. and Goel, M.L. (1977) *Political participation*. Chicago: Rand McNally.

Mirel, J. (2002, Summer) The decline of civic education. *Daedalus*, 49-55.

New York Times (1997) "Are Teachers of Teachers Out of Touch?," October 22.

Nye, J.S., Jr. (1997, Fall) In government we don't trust. Foreign Policy, 99-111.

Nye, J.S., Jr., P.D. Zelikow, and D.C. King, eds. (1997) *Why people don't trust government*. Cambridge: Harvard University Press.

Parker, Walter (2003) *Teaching democracy: Unity and diversity in public life*. New York: Teachers College Press.

Patterson, T.E. (2002a, August 25) Disappearing act. *Boston Globe*, p. D1.

Patterson, T.E. (2002b) *The vanishing voter*. New York: Knopf.

Phillips, D.C. (1995) The good, the bad, and the ugly. *Educational Researcher*, 24, 5-12.

Plambeck, J. (2002, November 25) Volunteerism trumps politics for students. *St. Louis Post-Dispatch*, p. B1.

Putnam, R.D. (2000) *Bowling alone: The collapse and revival of American community*. New York: Simon and Schuster.

Ravitch, D. (2000) *Left back: A century of failed school reforms*. New York: Simon and Schuster.

Ravitch, D. (2002, Summer) Education after the culture wars. *Daedalus*, 5-21.

Remmers, H.H. (1957) *The American teenager*. Indianapolis: Bobbs-Merrill.

Rochester, J.M. (2002) *Class warfare: Besieged schools, bewildered parents, betrayed kids, and the attack on excellence*. San Francisco: Encounter Books.

Rosenau, J.N. (1990) *Turbulence in world politics*. Princeton: Princeton University Press.

Russett, B. and H. Starr (1996) *World politics: menu for choice* (5th ed.). San Francisco: W.H. Freeman.

St. Louis Post-Dispatch (1995, November 3) Don't know much about history, p. C16.

Sansone, S. (1999, May/June) Get your students involved in civics. *Social Education*, 63, 228-232.

Schlesinger, A.M. (1992) *The disuniting of America*. New York: W.W. Norton.

Sengputa, S. (1997, October 22) Are teachers of teachers out of touch? *New York Times*, p. B8.

Shanker, A. (1996a, January 14) Knowledge still counts. *New York Times*.

Shanker, A. (1996b, December 29) Remembering teachers. *New York Times*.

Singer, A.J. (1997) *Social studies for secondary schools*. Mahwah, NJ: Lawrence Erlbaum Associates.

Sizer, T. (1984) *Horace's compromise—the dilemma of the American high school*. Boston: Houghton Mifflin.

Sorokin, E. (2002, August 19) NEA delivers history lesson. *Washington Times*, p. 1.

Stille, A. (2001, November 3) Suddenly, Americans trust Uncle Sam. *New York Times*, p. B9.

Stotsky, S. (1999) *Losing our language*. New York: Free Press.

Sykes, C. (1995) *Dumbing down our kids: Why America's children feel good about themselves but can't read, write, or add*. New York: St. Martins Press.

Uchitelle, L. (2000, May 5) Lonely bowlers, Unite: Mend the social fabric. *New York Times*, p. B9.

Verba, S. and N. Nie, (1972) *Participation in America: Political democracy and social equality*. New York: Harper and Row.

White, T. (2002, August 4) Howard's futuristic school. *Baltimore Sun*, p. B6.

Wilentz, S. (1998, April 20) The past is not a process. *New York Times*, p. A15.

Will, G.F. (2002, August 25) The feel-good approach to September 11. *Washington Post*.

Willis, S. (1995) Responding to public opinion. *Education Update* (June), p. 5.

Wilson, J.Q. and J.J. Dilulio. (1998) *American government: Institutions and politics* (7th ed.). Boston: Houghton Mifflin.

Wineburg, S. (2001) *Historical thinking and other unnatural acts*. Philadelphia: Temple University Press.

Yoder, E. (1996, January 10) Civilization's legacy of riches from dead white males. *St. Louis Post- Dispatch*, p. B7.

Zevin, J. (2000) *Social studies for the twenty-first century*. Mahwah, NJ. Lawrence Erlbaum Associates.

3

The Student, the World, and the Global Education Ideology

Jonathan Burack

The attack on America on September 11, 2001, led to a patriotic revival of sorts. Flags appeared on cars and front porches, Ordinary working heroes of the day—rescue workers, police officers, and fire fighters—were celebrated and honored. A new seriousness marked the opening ceremonies of sports events. And the nation appeared to rally to George W. Bush's vigorous call to arms against a new kind of totalitarian evil and threat to civilization. Much of this same spirit was also visible in classrooms and schools across the country. If the goal of the suicidal hijackers was to sow seeds of self-doubt, despair, and defeat among the population, it appeared their efforts had backfired. Instead, new confidence in American values and institutions could be detected just about everywhere.

Yet among the leadership of the social studies profession, a quite different mood was apparent. In the initial response to 9/11 in the pages of *Social Education* (the premier journal of the National Council for the Social Studies), on the website of the National Education Association, and in countless other rapidly assembled curriculum supplements, a clear effort was made to temper patriotic expressions in class and stress instead a need for therapeutic healing. The main concern was for the psyches of children who may have been traumatized by the horrendous and dramatically televised carnage. As for teaching anything of political or historical relevance, two overriding themes were almost instantly brought front and center: a need for students to practice tolerance toward Muslims and Arabs, and a need for students to look more critically at U.S. policy in the Middle East in order to better understand the motives of the attackers (Education Development Center, 2002; Finn, 2001; Simpson, 2001).

This focus shocked many Americans, as was clear from the instantaneous and all but universal bad press the NEA earned when one of its lessons suggested that teachers avoid placing blame on anyone for the attacks (Sorokin, 2002; Feldman, 2002). Yet no one should have been shocked. Anyone aware of the long-standing consensus among social studies professional elites on matters pertaining to world history or world cultures could have anticipated that these elites would do exactly what they did: harp on American insensitivity toward Islam while muting concerns about the murderous intolerance of Islamic radicals toward America. For two decades, and especially since the end of the Cold War, a global education ideology has taken hold in social studies education. This ideology, the international equivalent of separatist versions of multiculturalism, is deeply suspicious of America's institutions, values, and role in the world, while uncritically celebrating the institutions and values of most other societies. This ideology was clearly guiding many educators as they organized lessons and materials about 9/11 and its significance.

Before detailing this ideology and its curricular manifestations, it needs to be pointed out that rank-and-file teachers usually soften the ideology as they cope with the practical tasks of teaching about the world beyond our shores. Furthermore, among the population at large, this critical view of America and nonjudgmental stance toward America's enemies appear to have had little effect. If anything, the mindless mantra of tolerance at all costs may be triggering an understandable, if in some cases equally mindless, reaction against it (Waldman and Caldwell, 2002).

GLOBAL EDUCATION AND WORLD HISTORY: RECENT TRENDS

In recent years, the pressure to expand schools' coverage of world cultures, global education, and non-Western societies has been building. By itself, this trend is to be welcomed. Since World War II, America's role in the world has expanded enormously. If anything, the end of the Cold War has added to the burdens and responsibilities the role imposes. As the only superpower, the United States influences every other part of the globe. Even its inaction leads to awesome consequences everywhere. In addition, an increasingly globalized trading system is bringing a vastly more interconnected world into being. Political and economic linkages are supplemented and augmented now by many other cross-cultural and cross-national forces. On the level of popular culture, for instance, America's impact on others is far more profound than in the past. Finally, a new wave of immigration since the 1960s has brought to our own shores a far more diverse mix of peoples. For all these reasons, the impulse to teach students more about the rest of the world was inevitable and desirable.

Much less desirable is the fact that a troubling ideological agenda is driving this effort. This ideology needs to be identified and examined if an otherwise worthy education project is not to become merely another vehicle for politicizing the curriculum. Three central features of this ideology will be examined here under the headings of "multicultural celebration," "cultural relativism," and "transnational progressivism." First, though, it may help to look at how teaching and curriculum materials in the fields of world cultures and world history are changing.

Perhaps the most dramatic evidence of the growing emphasis on world history and culture is the new Advanced Placement World History course, which in 2001 took its place alongside familiar AP courses on U.S. and European history. The World History course focuses heavily on non-Western societies. No more than 30 percent of its content will be on the West (College Entrance Examination Board, 2001, p. 7). Just as important is its stress on broad social, cultural, and economic trends and cross-cultural comparisons at the expense of a narrative of events, personalities, and key moments of individual and collective decision making. By organizing itself this way, AP World History, an otherwise reasonable idea, could well accelerate harmful trends in the teaching of world history by promoting the global education ideology to be examined here.

As with any world history course, the new AP course must confront the problem of coverage: how to combine breadth with depth.

If students are not to be overwhelmed with massive amounts of detail, clear unifying principles must be employed to select the facts, nations, and trends to be stressed. Yet without some richness of detail, such coverage will be impossibly general and superficial. The AP course attempts to solve this problem by focusing on a few key themes (global interaction, change and continuity, technology, social structure, gender, etc.). The goal is to unify and structure the vast body of information about world history under these themes. This makes some sense. Yet the goal is made vastly more difficult to achieve because of another agenda: multiculturalism. The drive to cover all cultures equally adds enormously to the coverage problem by imposing an impossibly broad reach to the course. Moreover, by restricting coverage of the West, the course rejects what could provide a unifying principle for world history, at least for the past 500 years—namely, the central role of the West throughout the world.

The thematic approach of the AP course also results in a downplaying of politics. As the AP course description puts it, "Knowledge of year-to-year political events is not required. The traditional political narrative is an inappropriate model for this course" (College Entrance Examination Board, 2001, p. 7). Combined with limited coverage of the West, this means students will learn very little about the constitutional and political history out of which their own civic culture and institutions arose. The reduced attention to politics also mutes attention to the most important way in which individual human agency acts to drive human experience.

Contributing to this result is the de-emphasis on the role of nation-states in human affairs as opposed to broader cultural and geographic regions or, as the AP guide puts it, "the major civilizations in Africa, the Americas, Asia, and Europe." The slighting of the liberal democratic nation-state is another key feature of the global education ideology. The organizers of AP World History say, in effect, that the past 1,000 years of history consist of "processes that, over time, have resulted in the knitting of the world into a tightly integrated whole" (College Entrance Examination Board, 2001, p. 4). In a sense, this is a truism. But recent events should warn us about taking it too far. Our "tightly integrated" world system has not yet found a way to overcome deep religious, political, and cultural divisions. Nor does it appear to have found a way to dispense with nation-states as the preeminent players on the world stage or as the most important protectors—and violators—of constitutional government and liberty. Downplaying the nation-state's role in history is not yet justified by evidence either from the past or the present. It is an expression of ideology, not historical scholarship.

By demanding more of students, AP teachers may be able to handle the problems of coverage and depth. Such teachers are also likely to include plenty of politics and political theory, since it is hard to imagine how any competent history teacher could ignore them. Moreover, an AP European History course does still exist. But will it thrive? And how will the AP's prestige and influence affect the less rigorous courses in world history and global education that serve the majority of students?

Whatever the answer to these questions, it is clear that such courses already suffer greatly from the problems of breadth, depth, and the need to treat all cultures equally. Adding to these problems is the fact that world history, world cultures, and geography are often taught in the sixth or seventh grade (sometimes with follow-up world history courses in ninth or tenth grade). Under any circumstances, educators would have to simplify the subject for this young audience. But the pressure to cover all cultures equally, while offending none, vastly complicates the process of selecting material. It often results in courses consisting of little more than a smattering of geography, history, current events, and "cultural" analysis spread evenly across the globe.

The quotation marks around the word "cultural" in the last sentence are meant to indicate how vapid and inconsistent the term often is in world cultures curriculum materials. Any worthwhile world cultures course needs a systematic concept of culture taught and then used consistently to compare societies. Such a concept would define and explain linkages among family structure, kinship grouping, language, technology, religion, art, and ethical norms and laws. Far more common, however, is a seemingly random selection of disparate elements that are often superficial or exotic: clothing styles, food, holidays, religious observances, leisure activities, rituals, and other customs (see, for example, Bennetta, 1995). More often than not, such features are stressed mainly to provide a sense of difference and to "celebrate diversity," without much context to give them real meaning. Rarely is anything included that might strike a typical Western student as objectionable, e.g. female circumcision, slavery in Sudan, China's one-child policies, or religious discrimination (Kengor, 2002). In addition, the term "culture" itself is often used in confusing and inconsistent ways, at times referring to a region, a nation, a language group, a religion, or various racial, ethnic, and tribal groups within a nation. What often appears to govern the choice is an underlying victim-group/oppressor-group framework that, as we shall see, is yet another element in the global education ideology distorting this field and preventing it from developing coherence and rigor.

One final trend is worth commenting on, though it is still largely university based. This is the movement to internationalize the study and teaching of U.S. history. As with AP World History, a good case can be made for doing more to set U.S. history in a broad global context. Like every other nation, the United States has always existed in such a context, but it has become far more directly enmeshed in an international order since World War II. It is understandable, therefore, that historians might want to pay more attention to America's relationship to that order over the entire course of its history. The rationale for globalizing U.S. history teaching is spelled out in *The La Pietra Report: A Report to the Profession* (Bender, 2000). This report is a product of a four-year project by a group of historians assembled by the Organization of American Historians to rethink American history for a global age.

The *La Pietra* participants call for much more attention both to global contexts and to cross-cultural comparisons in U.S. history courses. They also urge historians to adopt various thematic frames of reference to supplement or even replace the nation-state. Finally, they seek to counter history teaching that might foster a sense of American "exceptionalism"—any notion, that is, that the United States has a unique history or role that students especially need to appreciate. On this point, the report says:

> By contextualizing the nation and comparing it with other
> nations one may better appraise the nature of its particu-
> lar, even exceptional qualities, while avoiding simplistic
> assertions of American exceptionalism (Bender, 2000,
> p. 3).

No one should quarrel with this way of putting it. What is odd, however, is the implication that U.S. history as presently taught is rife with simplistic assertions of American exceptionalism designed to pump students up with nationalistic pride. In fact, one would be hard pressed to find, say, a recent secondary school history textbook that does any such thing. Odd also is the implication that teachers today fail to set U.S. history in a global context—as if, for instance, they do not already routinely situate American colonial history in the larger context of an age of exploration and growing global interaction, or place the American Revolution in the context of the English and European Enlightenment, or set American slavery within the larger context of the Atlantic slave trade and the slave systems of Africa, the Caribbean, and the American continents.

In other words, the problems the *La Pietra* project claims to address do not appear to be all that significant. This suggests that other agendas might be at work. On the matter of American excep-tionalism, for instance, is the aim to temper uncritical pro-American bias, or is it to instill indifference to any patriotic appeal at all, no matter how well founded? After all, there are good grounds for fostering some forms of patriotic pride in students—with respect to our institutions of constitutionally-based liberty and democracy, for example. Does the movement to globalize U.S. his-tory hope to eliminate all such sentiments from the history classes? Some of the language in the report does suggest this sort of hostil-ity toward any positive portrayal of America and its role in the world today. At one point the *La Pietra* report warns that even inter-nationalized U.S. history courses will miss the real point if, by focusing on America's expanded global role, they "unthinkingly produce a form of historiographical imperialism or an ideological justification for globalization and American hegemony" (Bender, 2000, p. 3). The aim, then, is not just globalized U.S. history, but a version that weans students from an unacceptable celebratory stance toward their society or from any readiness to justify its "hegemonic" role in the world today. Such an agenda is one of political advocacy, not historical scholarship.

IS THERE A GLOBAL EDUCATION IDEOLOGY?

It is the central contention of this essay that a global education ideology does exist, developed and driven in part by a powerful confluence of institutional forces: key professional associations such as NCSS, NEA, and the World History Association; professors in schools of education; a number of institutes and foundations dedicated to promoting a global education agenda; and textbook companies with their teams of multicultural advisers and consultants who ensure that instructional materials serve the ideology's key purposes. Groups vigorously advocating for global education include the American Forum for Global Education and Global Education Associates in New York; Global Citizens for Change, a website project funded by the Ontario Ministry of Citizenship; Choices for the 21st Century Education Project at Brown University; the Stanford Program on International and Cross-Cultural Education (SPICE); the "Workable Peace" curriculum project of the Consensus Building Institute in Cambridge, Massachusetts; and many other university programs in international relations, global change, or human rights. Obviously, not all of these organizations buy into every aspect of the global education ideology outlined here, but many appear to be inspired by its basic spirit. Three elements of this ideology are key.

• **Multicultural Celebration:** An all-pervasive focus on the concept of "cultural diversity" and the need to expose students to as much of it as possible. This focus does help counter a traditional overemphasis on Western societies and an ethnocentric bias in the treatment of other societies. In recent years, however, textbooks and curricula have overcorrected for these defects. Nevertheless, many educators still insist that a pro-Western bias infects the teaching of world history and world cultures. In the meantime, their mantra of diversity for diversity's sake today is adding to already acute problems of excessive breadth of coverage and superficiality of treatment in global education curricula.

• **Cultural Relativism:** Global education advocates seek to promote respect and sympathetic understanding across cultures. This is all to the good. But true respect and sympathy cannot be based on a completely relativistic approach to culture, even though such an approach appears to dominate thinking in the field. By discouraging students who might wish to criticize negative aspects of other cultures, teachers seek to suppress what is likely an irrepressible natural human tendency to make moral judgments. Such pressure and hectoring probably foster cynicism and indifference in students, not a true spirit of tolerance.

• **Transnational Progressivism:** John Fonte (2001) of the Hudson Institute recently coined this term to refer to a tendency hostile to the liberal democratic nation-state and its claims to sovereignty. Fonte suspects that its aim is to redefine "democracy from a system of majority rule among equal citizens to power sharing among ethnic groups composed of both citizens and noncitizens" (Fonte, 2001, p. 3). Transnational progressives endorse a concept of post-national (global) citizenship and seek to shift authority to an institutional network of international organizations and subnational political actors not bound within any clear democratic, constitutional framework. In the global education field, this view is not dominant among rank-and-file teachers or even in the way textbooks get constructed. But it is a dynamic theme pushing the field forward. Those who embrace it are not content with a mere multicultural celebration of diverse societies and cultures. They see this "essentialist" view of distinct cultures as insufficiently global and focus instead on global trends, transnational cultural interchanges, and worldwide problems, especially those that can be depicted as rendering the nation-state obsolete.

GLOBAL EDUCATION IDEOLOGY: CONTRADICTIONS

The global education ideology outlined above does not provide a coherent strategy for curriculum development nor an instructional theory able to guide teachers in organizing and teaching lessons. In part, this is because the ideology's advocates have political objectives they do not openly acknowledge. And in part it is because the ideology is internally incoherent and contradictory. That is, it claims to support things that in fact will be harder to accomplish because of it. What follows is a brief look at the key contradictions.

A MULTICULTURALISM THAT IS NEITHER "MULTI" NOR "CULTURAL"

In a recent review of world history textbooks used in Wisconsin, Paul Kengor (2002) found substantial attention devoted to the internment of Japanese-Americans in the U.S. during World War II. At the same time, he found little space devoted to Japan's treatment of POWs and other Japanese atrocities in the war, in particular the murder and rape-murder of hundreds of thousands of civilians in Nanking in 1937 (Kengor, pp. 10-11).

What are we to make of this imbalance, in which far less attention is paid to the far more horrifying injustice? What is especially striking is that these are *world* history texts. Would it not have made more sense for them to focus on Japan's actions in the war rather than U.S. home-front policies? After all, U.S. history textbooks already do quite well indeed in covering the Japanese-American internment.

This imbalance illustrates the contradictions of multiculturalism as it is enshrined now in educational practice. Japan is home to a culturally distinct people quite different from the vast majority of Americans. It would have been a worthwhile multicultural exercise to ask students to consider whether the Japanese atrocities revealed something about Japanese culture in general or were simply a result of the dictatorial political regime ruling Japan at that time. On the other hand, the Japanese-Americans of the internment camps were, by and large, not a distinct and separate culture. They were mainly U.S. citizens whose ethnic heritage shaped some aspects of their lives but who for the most part had adapted to and internalized the norms and patterns of American society. Nevertheless, world history textbook writers apparently see this Japanese-American ethnic group as far more worthy than Japan itself of multicultural "inclusion."

Why? To put it simply, multiculturalism has less to do with any rigorous study of other cultures than with ethnic, gender, racial, or other subgroup tension within the nations of the West, the United States in particular. Lacking a clear, consistent, and nonideological definition of culture, global education advocates and other proponents of multiculturalism exhibit a strong tendency to identify such subgroups as "cultures," especially when they can be depicted as victims of a "dominant culture." The result is that students are taught to view the world not as multicultural but as bicultural—as a world of oppressed vs. oppressor. A key corollary is the view of the West as the region where such subgroup "cultures" have been most grievously oppressed.

THE UNBEARABLE BLANDNESS OF DIVERSITY

McDougal Littell's *Modern World History: Patterns of Interaction* is a popular world history textbook (Beck, 1999). Under a heading of "History Through Art," a page in this book is devoted to African textiles. Colorful patterns of cloth are displayed. An Ivory Coast chief is shown wearing Kente cloth. Brief paragraphs describe the various kinds of cloth and the "cultures" that produce them. The claim is made that historians can learn much from these fabrics about each group's myths, celebrations, and social roles. What students learn from this page, however, is a good deal less than that. Here is a typical paragraph, the one on Kuba cloth:

> Made by Kuba people of the Congo, this cloth was made of raffia, a palm-leaf fiber. The cloth design was based on traditional geometric styles. The cloth was worn at ceremonial events, was used as currency, and may have been offered for part of a dowry (Beck, p. 312).

This is very interesting. However, since the Kuba people are never again mentioned in the textbook, no possibility exists of finding out why geometric styles were used or what their symbolic meaning to the Kuba might be. No description of Kuba "ceremonial events" is offered. Nor is the Kuba economy described or Kuba family structure analyzed, hence the significance of Kuba cloth as currency or as part of a dowry goes unexamined. The page is located in the middle of a chapter titled, "The Age of Imperialism, 1850-1914." The information on this page is connected neither to the chapter's historical theme nor to any overall concept of culture that might explain the artifacts depicted. Moreover, nowhere else in the book are textiles from any other region illustrated and described in this way, hence no useful cross-cultural comparisons are possible.

This is multiculturalism as a kind of exotic and colorful ethnic travelogue. It serves no significant educational purpose. Its location in the chapter on imperialism may be intended to reinforce a victim-group/oppressor (Africa/Europe) framework. But the primary purpose appears to be to get students to recognize the achievements of the various African peoples mentioned. The cloth patterns are indeed striking. As with so much multicultural material, the goal is to teach students to celebrate diversity and appreciate other cultures.

But "celebrating" and "appreciating" are not the same thing. This African textiles "lesson" is based on a progressive educational approach that equates raw experience with learning. However, the material does little to extend the visual experience of colorful patterns of cloth into any substantive knowledge or understanding. The teacher's edition of the text suggests several activities, none of which entails learning anything about the societies that made the fabrics. One activity, based on Howard Gardner's multiple intelligences theory, is directed at "kinesthetic learners" (Beck, p. 313). It suggests that such students get help from the art teacher in tie-dying textiles of their own, using modern-day cloth and "nontoxic commercial dyes," of course. What this is meant to teach about African textiles, African cultures, or the history of imperialism is (mercifully) left unstated.

This African textile lesson is found in a high school world history textbook. As a lesson type, it is somewhat of an exception in that book (which nevertheless has many other problems). However, it is absolutely typical of the approach to culture found in less demanding world history and world cultures materials, especially for middle school students. It exemplifies a stunningly superficial treatment of stylistic cultural differences around the world. To avoid giving offense, only uplifting aspects of any culture are normally stressed. When something unpleasant is dealt with, it is done so indirectly, vaguely, and only if it can be presented within an acceptable muliticulturalist framework.

An especially odd example appears on page 549 of McDougal Littell's *World Cultures and Geography* (Bednarz, 2003). This page includes a brief paragraph on Rwanda. The paragraph, headed "Government in Rwanda," is about events there in the 1990s. One would naturally expect the passage to deal with the tensions between the Hutu and Tutsi tribes and the tragic way in which they led to one of the worst slaughters in history. In its defense, the book does very briefly mention these events earlier, on page 511. However, on page 549, it gives them a very peculiar spin:

> In 1991, a new constitution was passed. It gave women the right to own property and hold jobs. But the new laws were not enforced. Then, in 1994, a civil war began in Rwanda. So many men were killed that women began taking over as heads of households. Finally, as a result of the deadly wars, women were able to claim their constitutional rights (Bednarz, p. 549).

Amazingly, this passage turns one of the century's worst acts of genocide into a "civil war" that inadvertently advanced the rights of women! The irony is that it defeats entirely the objective of exposing students to true cultural diversity. Instead of wrestling in any deep way with the nature of tribal, ethnic, and gender conflict in Africa, students are invited to view these events through a far more familiar lens, that of women's struggles for "constitutional rights."

Even the issue of women's rights in Rwanda is itself unlikely to be understood outside of a modern Western frame without much more historical background on women in Rwanda than students get from this textbook. And this is the key point about the blandness of diversity. Without solid historical context *and* a strong grounding in their own Western cultural heritage, students will not be able to grasp fully how other cultures differ. To understand the role of women in Rwanda, for instance, one needs to know what ideas prevail there about the relationship generally of the individual to family, community, and state. Moreover, to fully appreciate these relationships as "different" from their own, students also need some awareness of Western ideas about the individual's relationship to authority as these have evolved from feudalism and the Magna Carta, to Locke and Jefferson, to the "Declaration of the Rights of Man and the Citizen," and on to Seneca Falls and the modern women's rights movement. An uncritical celebration of multiculturalism cannot provide this context. It cannot lead to a true appreciation of cultural difference. In fact, it will only mire students further in a bland and smug satisfaction with their own (or their teachers') notions about such matters. Actually, even this textbook's earlier reference to Rwanda (Bednarz, p. 511) illustrates a related point. It describes the Hutu/Tutsi rivalry in the context of European imperialism, stressing the way colonial political rule exacerbated tensions between the two tribal groups. The student still learns nothing of the specific nature of these two groups, what the traditional fault lines between them were, and why colonial rule was able to intensify those fault lines so drastically or (given that colonial rule had ended well before 1994) over such a distance in time.

TOLERATING THE INTOLERANCE OF THE "OTHER"

The relativist stance so common in the global education field today constitutes a refusal to apply any universal ethical standards in judging another culture. Yet this denial of universal standards is itself a universal standard, usually called "tolerance." Tolerance is an admirable quality. But if it is our sole universal value, are we not then called upon to tolerate the intolerable? And if so called upon, are we even capable of performing such an act of mental jujitsu? In fact, the pressure not to apply moral standards is more likely to produce an ethic of "indifference" than one of true tolerance—as young people learn not to pass judgment on all kinds of horrendous practices, especially when they are non-Western. In trying to suppress what is probably a natural human tendency (to judge), these students are more likely to become morally numb, certainly not "sensitive" to the "Other." The widely recognized political disengagement of young people today may, in part, reflect this aspect of their training.

Another way to handle the challenge of tolerating the intolerable is denial. This has certainly characterized the response of many educators to the post-9/11 threat of Islamic radicalism. In countless ways, such educators have insisted on misinforming students about this threat by denying its links to any aspect of Islam as a religion or to the Islamic societies of the Middle East and Asia. And when such links cannot be ignored (as, for example, the horrendous treatment of women by the Taliban or the rulers of Saudi Arabia, or the clear calls for war against the infidel by many Muslim clerics, or the widespread dissemination of Nazi-style, anti-Semitic propaganda throughout the Arab world), students are still exhorted to tolerate the intolerable by "understanding" its cultural or historical context to the point of excusing it.

Take the Islamic concept of *jihad*. Shahid Athar, a doctor and Islamic writer, responds on his website to questions about Islam. Here is what he has to say about *jihad*:

> The word "Jihad" means struggle, or to be specific, striving in the cause of God. Any struggle done in day-to-day life to please God can be considered Jihad. One of the highest levels of Jihad is to stand up to a tyrant and speak a word of truth. Control of the self from wrong doings is also a great Jihad. One of the forms of Jihad is to take up arms in defense of Islam or a Muslim country when Islam is attacked (retrieved at: http://islam-usa.com/25ques. html#14).

This statement could stand in for hundreds like it that have appeared lately on the Internet, in books and magazines, and in educational materials on the attacks of 9/11. Muslim organizations in America and global education advocates together have worked vigorously to promote the notion of Islam as a peaceful religion, and the notion of *jihad* as peaceful striving and self-improvement.

Unfortunately, the notion is largely false. This is not the place to go in depth into the relevant scholarship. Those who wish to do this might consult *Jihad in Classical and Modern Islam: A Reader*, by Peters (1996) or Pipes's (2002) article "Jihad and the Professors." It is true that a Sufi variant of the term *jihad* does resemble Dr. Athar's definition. But for most of Islam's history, the vast majority of Muslims, including scholars and religious leaders, have clearly understood *jihad* to mean primarily a war to expand and defend the realm of Islam.

This is so obviously the case that some educators resort to a sleight-of-hand in passing off the sanitized variant. Here, for example, is a definition provided in a lesson on Afghanistan in a recent issue of NCSS's *Social Education*:

> *JIHAD*: Arabic term meaning striving or effort in the service of God. It refers to an individual's struggle to overcome personal traits that are in conflict with the Koran. *It is often used* (italics added) to describe a war undertaken by Muslims as a sacred duty—a political or military struggle on behalf of Islam (Mertz, 2001, p. 435).

Students would never know from the passive construction of that last sentence that Muslims past and present all but universally accept the idea of *jihad* as a war to expand or defend the realm of Islam. They might even conclude that only Eurocentric Westerners see it that way. The redefinition of *jihad* as peaceful self-struggle is part of a more general tendency to soften Islam's harsher edges in dealing with it in world history and world cultures courses and curriculum materials. Such materials are now quite common and, due to vigorous advocacy by many Muslim groups in America, they are becoming still more common (Bennetta, 2002). What these groups ought to consider is that they may actually be defeating their own stated purpose of promoting greater understanding. As one writer puts it, "If we stifle rational discussion of Islam, what will emerge will be the very thing that political correctness and the government seek to avoid: virulent, racist populism" (Warraq, 2002).

After all, students need not immerse themselves in historical study to come to doubt the validity of these euphemisms about *jihad*. They have the evidence of the daily news. *Jihad* as peaceful self-struggle, as Pipes notes, contradicts the headlines students see every day:

> It suggests that Osama bin Laden had no idea what he was saying when he declared jihad on the United States several years ago and then repeatedly murdered Americans in Somalia, at the U.S. embassies in East Africa, in the port of Aden, and then on September 11, 2001. It implies that organizations with the word "jihad" in their titles, including Palestinian Islamic Jihad and bin Laden's own "International Islamic Front for the Jihad Against Jews and Crusade[rs]," are grossly misnamed. And what about all the Muslims waging violent and aggressive jihads, under that very name and at this very moment, in Algeria, Egypt, Sudan, Chechnya, Kashmir, Mindanao, Ambon, and other places around the world? (Pipes, 2002, p. 19).

Another key Islamic term often whitewashed in this way is that of *dhimmitude*, the term for the subordinate status of Christians, Jews, and other religious groups in Muslim lands. Most secondary school textbooks and other materials routinely characterize *dhimmitude* as a "protected" status under which non-Muslims were treated with tolerance and allowed to maintain their own religious traditions. There is some basis for putting things this way, and it may well be that religious minorities in other cultures suffered worse treatment at times. Yet the fact remains that *dhimmitude* was a form of religious discrimination, and not a pleasant one. It could be compared to "Jim Crow" segregation in the U.S. South, though the work of some scholars might lead one to view even this comparison as too kind (Bat Ye'or, 1996). Ironically, while presenting *dhimmitude* as a form of tolerance, secondary school world history texts also often heap praise on the Muslim emperor Akbar in Moghul India for his tolerance in abolishing many aspects of *dhimmitude*, including the *jizya*, the poll tax imposed on religious minorities elsewhere in the ancient Muslim world. Left unclear is exactly how both *dhimmitude* and the abolition of *dhimmitude* are examples of "tolerance."

What accounts for this unwillingness to deal honestly with unpleasant truths about Islam? After all, most of the educators who deny any link between Islam and violence or Islam and the harsh treatment of women are perfectly happy to take note of similar facts about Christianity's past. Few textbooks today slight the Crusades, the Inquisition, the wars of religion, the persecution of witches, the arrogance of missionaries, and much else. In fact, dwelling on such defects is seen as a necessary corrective to past Eurocentric bias in world history materials and courses. This glaring double standard arises out of the troubling contradiction in global education ideology described here as tolerance of the intolerable. Because of it, many global education and world history programs overlook or whitewash forms of injustice and brutality in other cultures that they roundly denounce in Western societies.

CITIZENSHIP WITHOUT SOVEREIGNTY: THE MAKING OF GLOBAL CITIZENS

The ideal of "global citizenship" is much touted in the recent literature on global education and world history. This ideal often amounts to little more than an appeal for students to show concern about such matters as environmental degradation, worldwide poverty, or AIDS in Africa. For some, however, the term is meant more literally and radically. These advocates claim that the traditional liberal democratic nation-state has failed and that membership in such a state must ultimately be augmented by a new, more encompassing, global citizenship. In a statement written for the American Forum for Global Education, for example, Collins, Czarra, and Smith tell us:

> Since the end of the Cold War, new forces—cultural, political, environmental, and economic—have swept the world. Americans are reexamining the role of their country within these new global complexities and questioning the ability of many of our basic institutions from the government to the military to our financial institutions to cope with these new realities (Collins, Czarra, and Smith; 1996; p. 1).

Is it in fact true that Americans are questioning the ability of our "basic" institutions to cope with the new realities of a global world order? Certainly, millions of Americans realize that we live in a more interconnected world. And they know full well that this new world contains daunting challenges to us as a nation. But what evidence is there of lack of confidence in our institutions? When the attacks of 9/11 occurred, Americans did not look to the UN, the European Union or any other transnational entity to cope. They looked to the U.S. president, the Congress, the military, and other purely American institutions, as well as to themselves as individuals. For the most part, they still appear to be doing this, however much they may carp about this or that aspect of the way these institutions have responded.

Clearly, however, many global education advocates want Americans to doubt the ability of their national civil society and its government to deal with global challenges. Global Education Associates posts this claim prominently on its website: "GEA's work in redefining sovereignty and security constitutes one of the more enlightened initiatives to world peace based on long-term and structural dynamics" (Giardino, n.d., para 9). This missionary drive to redefine sovereignty inspires much global education literature. The American Forum for Global Education devoted an entire issue of one of its recent newsletters to excerpting parts of what is described as a classic in the field (Lee F. Anderson's *Schooling and Citizenship in a Global Age: An Exploration of the Meaning and Significance of Global Education,* Bloomington, Indiana: Mid-America Program for Global Perspectives in Education, Social Studies Development Center, 1979). In American Forum's excerpts, Anderson depicts globalization not simply as a stepped-up process of greater interrelatedness among nations and societies, but as a new stage of history that transcends the nation-state:

> The progressive globalization of the human condition has produced a social system that is larger and more inclusive than nations, and this world system can be fruitfully conceptualized as a global society (Anderson, 2000-2001, p. 3).

Anderson goes on to define the concept of global citizenship that he feels is needed now that we all live in a "common global culture."

Citizenship refers to the decisions, the judgments, and the actions through which individuals link themselves—knowingly or unknowingly, deliberately and inadvertently—to the public affairs of the groups of which they are members (Anderson, 2000-2001, p. 13)

In one sense, this definition is so broad as to be almost without content. Yet that is what makes it useful to advocates of global citizenship. Its vague reference to the many "groups" to which individuals belong severs the link between the citizen and a single, overarching national civic community. At the same time, these multiple groups compete for each citizen's loyalties, encouraging a balkanization in which subgroups, not individual citizens, become the essential units of the social order. This combination of enhanced subgroup authority and diminished national sovereignty is precisely the agenda of what Fonte identifies as "transnational progressivism."

But can citizenship in fact float freely in this way, unhinged from any sovereign national authority? In the liberal democratic state, such sovereign authority derives ultimately from the people. Effective democratic citizenship requires at minimum a dependable constitutional order protecting basic human rights and providing for elections, freedom of expression, and open debate, and the ability of loyal opponents of the government to organize and compete freely for power. Participation as a citizen means above all the right to ratify the decisions of the government regularly through elections and to change leaders when necessary. In the global education literature, such acts of ratification are not stressed. Instead, global citizens are more often exhorted simply to work through various civil society organizations or nongovernmental organizations (NGOs) and to put their faith in a vaguely defined "international community." Little emphasis is placed on how citizens will hold that international community accountable in a democratic way.

Fortunately, most serious scholars of international relations deal with the issue of global interconnectedness far more soberly than do advocates of the global education ideology. While such scholars acknowledge the growing entanglement of nation-states in an expanding web of international agreements and regimes, many of them doubt that the nation state is about to be replaced. In his book *Sovereignty: Organized Hypocrisy*, Stephen Krasner (1999) develops the thesis that states have never enjoyed absolute sovereignty, even though they all act as if they have it (hence, the "hypocrisy" in the title of the book). Limits on sovereignty, in other words, are not new. They shift in response to changing conditions. But for the foreseeable future they are unlikely to end the central role of national power and national interest in determining the behavior of the international order.

Even some who view these globalizing trends favorably also acknowledge their darker side. Writing in *Foreign Affairs*, Jessica Mathews hopes that the diffusion of nation-state power will "mean more peace, justice, and capacity to manage the burgeoning list of humankind's interconnected problems." Yet she admits there are "at least as many reasons, however, to believe that the continuing diffusion of power away from nation-states will mean more conflict and less problem solving both within states and among them" (Mathews, 1997, p. 64). Writing in a different context, Daniel Brumberg (2002) makes a telling point about the value of a coherent, constitutionally grounded democratic state. Speaking of flaws in what he calls the "liberal autocracy" of many Middle East nations, he says:

> By themselves, civil society organizations cannot make up for the lack of a functioning political society, meaning an autonomous realm of self-regulating political parties that have the constitutional authority to represent organized constituencies in parliaments (Brumberg, 2002, p. 64).

Yet advocates of global citizenship rarely go beyond a call for greater reliance on civil society organizations acting through various unaccountable or semi-accountable international bodies. Such a program would undermine the real basis for active citizenship the constitutional, democratic nation-state. Ironically, this would not be likely to produce the more involved citizens these advocates say they seek. It would more likely produce passive subjects of an unaccountable international order.

Adding to this likelihood is global education's willful de-emphasis of the West, especially its political history, and minimizing of decisive individuals and great leaders. The stress is instead on social and cultural trends, and on non-Western and "marginalized" voices and stories. As a result, less attention is paid to the foundations of Western political freedom, from ancient Greece to the Magna Carta, the Glorious Revolution, the Enlightenment, and the American and French Revolutions. Kengor (2002, p. 9) points out that world-historical figures such as Churchill, Napoleon, Luther, Hitler, Lenin, and Lincoln are downplayed in favor of cultural icons and protest voices (Mother Teresa, Olaudah Equiano, Rigoberta Menchu). The result is a bias against the role of the individual in history, since those individuals who are described are often included as representatives of groups, usually victimized or "marginalized" groups, or to illustrate traditions of reactive protest against key decision-makers rather than the decision-makers themselves. The Western political tradition can only be grasped if the student becomes familiar with the ideas and lives of a large number of intellectual and political actors who happen mainly to be white males. Without this history, students will be taught a view of the past that centers not on individuals as the makers of history but on impersonal forces and helpless masses as the objects of history.

GLOBAL EDUCATION: "HARD" AND "SOFT" APPROACHES

The most committed proponents of the global education ideology outlined here are activists with an agenda. They explicitly seek to wean American students from a "retrograde" loyalty to the nation-state and refocus them on a globalist agenda that is hostile to the West. Just beneath the surface of much of the cutting edge literature in the field lies a view of the West—and the United States in particular—as a malevolent political and cultural force. Expressing this spirit in a somewhat light-hearted way, one global education organization recently published a poem titled "The United States of Borg" which begins this way:

> We are the United States of Borg.
> You will be assimilated. Resistance is futile.
> We will assimilate your cultural and national
> distinctiveness into our own.
> You will be made to serve the process of globalization.
> You will adopt American values as your own
> (Jacobs, 2000).

Given this view of America's globalizing cultural and political impact, it is perhaps understandable that these advocates feel that a new anti-American global citizenship is called for. But do most world history or world cultures teachers agree with such views? No one can be sure, but it seems doubtful. The textbooks in the field, at least, do not depict the United States in such harsh terms. For the most part, a softer version of the ideology prevails and can be summed up by the catch phrase "celebrate diversity." This seems innocuous enough, but it results in a vapid, overly broad curriculum. It wastes students' time on such things as African textiles, ethnic holiday feasts, and American pop culture icons. But it is primarily motivated by a well-intended desire to have students learn about and appreciate other cultures as well as their own.

Both "hard" and "soft" proponents of global education tend to favor what they see as a more liberating and participatory pedagogy. They endorse the standard progressive education mantra against the supposedly rote "drill-and-kill" methods of an imagined authoritarian system. They see themselves as freeing children from a more rigidly conventional pedagogy focused on traditional subjects, and instead "involving" students in the construction of alternative views of the world and in more active and cooperative efforts to realize them.

Here again, however, the harder version of the ideology pushes this progressive pedagogy further. Take, for example, the desire to reconstruct subject-area boundaries. Advocating this is Ross Dunn, Director of World History Projects at the National Center for

History in the Schools at UCLA. He recently identified and evaluated several world history models (1999). The first is the traditional "Western Heritage Model," which stresses the history of the West and its institutions. Dunn has little good to say about this approach, though he praises its "dedication to democracy, freedom, and a shared system of cultural communication." This aside, he is harshly critical of the model's "essentialist point of view"—that is, its view of the West as carrying "inborn characteristics" constituting an "essential" core of values and ideas.

But Dunn is also unhappy with what he sees as the most popular alternative, which he calls the "Different Cultures Model." This model also views cultures as having inherent ("essential") characteristics, though it exposes students to a much wider range of such cultures. He credits the model's popularity to the "triumph of multiculturalism."

> That is, the multicultural tenets that world history education should be culturally inclusive, attentive to diversity, moderately relativist, internationally minded, and hostile to the idea that any single culture is inherently better or worse than any other have won acceptance, at least resigned acceptance, in virtually all state and large-city education agencies (Dunn, 1999, Introduction).

Dunn greatly prefers what he calls the "Patterns of Change Model." Like the "Different Cultures" model, this one is "socially and culturally inclusive." But it rejects the idea that the cultural, ethnic, or national groups described in history books are "solid, commonsensical, and agreed-upon" rather than "contested, uncertain, and in flux."

> The Patterns of Change Model advances the idea that social and spatial fields of historical inquiry should be open and fluid, not predetermined by fixed cultural or geographical categories. Structuring world history curriculum, then, is not so much a matter of deciding how to line up study of various autonomously conceived cultures

but of framing substantive, engaging historical questions that students might be invited to ask unconstrained by predetermined border lines of civilizations, nations, or continents (Dunn, Introduction).

This model, according to Dunn, requires world history materials to "start not with selection of places to study but with problems to investigate." Reflecting postmodern thinking, it seems perfectly designed to erode traditional subject-area boundaries and confuse students. It also tends to diminish the role of the nation-state.

A similarly disorienting tendency appears within the aforementioned *La Pietra* project to internationalize U.S. history teaching. Guarneri (2002), for example, suggests the use of transnational political, social, or environmental trends as the core organizing themes for an American history course. He then goes on to say:

> One can even imagine a future in which more aggressively globalized United States survey courses present the nation much more as a site than a subject, located near the midpoint between local, regional, continental, and global processes, not always the relevant unit of inquiry and only occasionally decisive as an historical intervener" (Guarneri, 2002, p. 46).

Given this approach, it is hard to see why a separate U.S. history course of any sort ought to be provided in the first place.

The hard version of the global education ideology combines a rejection of traditional subject-area content with deep skepticism about the political worth of the nation-state and support for a divisive, anti-Western form of multiculturalism. It claims to offer a broader, more tolerant approach to world culture and history. And, with its stress on a problem-centered rather than subject-centered curriculum, it claims to offer students a more active learning experience, one that will move them to participate as global citizens in building a better world. In fact, by suppressing the student's natural tendency to make—and to want to make—moral judgments, by relentlessly denigrating the student's core Western cultural heritage, and by pandering to the supposed victim status of some cultures in relation to others, this ideology is a recipe for further alienating a generation already too comfortable with a fashionable distrust of authority and consequent withdrawal into civic passivity and cynicism.

GLOBAL EDUCATION: CHANGING THE DIRECTION

It is unlikely that most teachers of world history and global cultures embrace the "hard" approach. Most world history textbooks, while including much more on non-Western cultures, still accept a conventional focus on regions, civilizations, and nations, and on traditional time-period frameworks. Most world culture textbooks consist of geography and regional studies carried out in fairly conventional ways. And most teachers still appear comfortable with these approaches. This "soft" version of the global education ideology does cause problems, to be sure, but these mainly have to do with excessive breadth of coverage and lack of rigor in the study or evaluation of other cultures. The blanket of political correctness all but guarantees that students will learn little of substantive value about other cultures or grapple meaningfully with the very diversity the ideology claims to celebrate. But because the harder-edged version of the ideology has not yet triumphed, there is reason to hope that a more open debate can result in change for the better. In attempting to further that debate, educators need to embrace what is sound in the shift to a more global perspective while carefully identifying and criticizing what is harmful. Here are a few suggestions for those who wish to do this.

• **Stress the continuing centrality of the West.** It needs to be made clear that the goal is not to celebrate the West's glories uncritically. It is to recognize, first, that the West has been the central force in world history for the past five centuries and, just as importantly, that the West is the source of the most important civic ideas and ideals that we want students to understand.

• **Include other cultures, but honestly—warts and all, East and West.** The multicultural ideal can only be honestly pursued if educators reject the double standard that judges the West harshly while ignoring the defects of other cultures. This does not mean the West's flaws should be minimized. It does mean they need to be set in the context of an honest appraisal of the flaws of other societies.

• **Note the contradictions of the global education ideology.** Demonstrate the failure of the ideology to achieve what its supporters believe it can achieve. This is especially true with regard to pressures on students to tolerate other cultures uncritically. If educators can come to see that the mantra of multicultural tolerance is likely to generate a contemptuous resistance among students, they may be more open to the idea of providing more honest and believable assessments of other cultures.

• **Stress the superficiality, inaccuracy, and blandness of "world cultures" and "world history" materials.** The mistakes commonly found in textbooks are a disgrace. One reason for them is the textbook-by-committee approach now made even more nightmarishly bureaucratic by the relentless pressures of identity politics and political correctness (Ravitch, 2003). This also explains the bland superficiality of so many of these resources. The point for educators is that this is a key source of boredom among their students. The faith that a celebratory multiculturalism will make social studies more appealing to a more diverse student body is misplaced. Instead, it yields a bland and manipulative approach that leaves students apathetic and cynical.

• **Encourage stronger narrative history with a focus on moral and political action.** This point needs to be made in conjunction with the previous one. Not only will this recommendation restore human agency to the central place it deserves in the telling of the human story. It will also move students in the only legitimate ways that history can move them—by exposing them to the decisive actions by which human beings shaped their past and the foregone choices by which they might have shaped it differently.

REFERENCES

Ahmad, I., et al. (2001). *World cultures: a global mosaic*. Upper Saddle River, NJ: Prentice Hall.

Athar, Shahid. In the name of God, most kind and most merciful. Retrieved at http://islam-usa.com/25ques.html#14.

Anderson, L.F. (2000-2001). Schooling and Citizenship in a Global Age. *Issues in Global Education* (No. 164), 1–19.

Beck, R.B., et al. (1999). *Modern world history: patterns of interaction*. Evanston, IL: McDougal Littell.

Bednarz, S.W., et. al. (2003). *World cultures and geography*. Evanston, IL. McDougal Littell.

Bender, T. (2000). Bloomington, IN: Organization of American Historians. Retrieved at http://www.oah.org/activities/lapietra/final.html.

Bennetta, W.J. (1995, May-June). Like the 1993 version, this book is worthless. *The textbook letter*. Retrieved at http://www.textbookleague.org/.

Bennetta, W.J. (2002). Houghton Mifflin's Islamic connection. *The textbook letter*. Retrieved at http://www.textbook league.org/.

Brumberg, D. (2002, October). The trap of liberalized autocracy. *Journal of Democracy*, 13(4), 56-68.

College Entrance Examination Board. (2001, May). *AP world history course description*. Retrieved at http://www.college-board.com/ap.

Collins, H.T., Czarra, F.R., and Smith, A.F. (1996). Guidelines for global and international studies education: challenges, culture, connections. *American Forum for Global Education*. Retrieved at http://www.globaled.org/guidelines/index.php.

Dunn, R. (1999). Contending definitions of world history: introduction. *Issues in Global Education*, 151. Retrieved at http://www.globaled.org/issues/151/index.html.

Education Development Center. (2002). *Beyond blame: reacting to the terrorist attack.* Retrieved at http://www.edc.org/spotlight/schools/beyondblame.htm.

Feldman, S. (2002) Statement by Sandra Feldman, President, American Federation of Teachers on Lesson Plans for September 11. Press Release. August 20, 2002. Retrieved at http://www.aft.org/press/2002/082002_911.html.

Finn, C.E. (2001, December). Teachers, terrorists, and tolerance. *Commentary*, 112(5). 54-57.

Fonte, J. (2001, October 26). Liberal democracy vs. transnational progressivism: the future of the ideological civil war within the west. Retrieved at http://www.hudson.org/index.cfm?fuseaction=publication_details&id=1008.

Giardino, T.F. (n.d.). Global Education Associates endorsements. Retrieved at http://www.globaleduc.org/endorsements.htm.

Guarneri, C.J. (2002, November). Internationalizing the United States survey course: American history for a global age. *The History Teacher*, 36(1), 37-64.

Jacobs, K. (2000). The United States of Borg, *Issues in Global Education* (158), American Forum for Global Education. Retrieved at http://www.globaled.org/issues/158/index.html.

Kengor, P. (2002). *Evaluating world history texts in Wisconsin public high schools.* Thiensville, WI: Wisconsin Policy Research Institute.

Krasner, S.D. (1999). *Sovereignty: Organized Hypocrisy.* Princeton, NJ: Princeton University Press.

Mathews, J.T. (1997, January/February). Power shift. *Foreign Affairs*, 76(1), 50-66.

Mertz, G. (2001) Civil war in Afghanistan. *Social Education*, 65(7), 429-436.

Peters, R. (1996). *Jihad in classical and modern islam: A Reader.* Princeton, NJ: Marcus Weiner.

Pipes, D. (2002, November). *Jihad* and the professors.

Commentary, 114(4), 17-21.

Ravitch, Diane (2003). *The language police: how pressure groups restrict what students learn*. New York: Alfred A. Knopf.

Simpson, M. (Ed.). (2001). Teaching about tragedy [special issue]. *Social Education* 65(6), 346-351.

Sorokin, E. (2002, August 19). NEA delivers history lesson. *Washington Times*. Retrieved at http://www.washtimes.com /national/.

Sorokin, E. (2002, August 20). NEA plan for 9/11 not backed by teachers. *Washington Times*. Retrieved at http://www.wash-times.com/national/.

Waldman, S. and Caldwell, D. (October 30, 2002).Unease with Islam: public opinion shifts, as religious leaders speak out. Special to ABC News.com. Retrieved at http://www.abcnews .go.com/sections/us/DailyNews/islam021028.html.

Warraq, I. (2002, November 10). Honest intellectuals must shed spiritual turbans. *The Guardian Unlimited*. Retrieved at http://www.guardian.co.uk/saturday_review/story/0,3605, 590647,00.html

Ye'or, Bat. (1996). *The decline of eastern Christianity under Islam: from jihad to dhimmitude*. London: Associated University Press.

4

Multiculturalism and Social Studies[1]

Lucien Ellington and Jana S. Eaton

"There is no room in this country for hyphenated Americans. . . . The one absolutely certain way of bringing this nation to ruin, of preventing all possibility of its continuing to be a nation at all, would be to permit it to become a tangle of squabbling nationalities."

—Theodore Roosevelt

Harvard sociologist Nathan Glazer (1997) named a recent book *We Are All Multiculturalists Now* because, in his opinion, "we all now accept a greater degree of attention to minorities and women and their role in American history and social studies and literature in schools" (pp. 13-14). Certainly there is little doubt that multicultural education has been institutionalized within social studies. Multicultural goals and content are present in schools' social studies curricula, states' social studies standards, and pre- and in-service social studies teacher education.

Before the 1960s, treatment of ethnicity and minorities in U.S. history and social studies left much to be desired, as these groups were either largely ignored or often subjected to negative stereotyping. America now is even more multiethnic than four decades ago. School history and social studies classes must include significant multicultural components. Serious study of the various ethnic groups that are part of our society is a necessity if we are to have a truly educated citizenry. The critical question is *what kind* of multicultural education is most appropriate for our children. Two visions seem to have emerged. "Cultural pluralism," while recognizing our differences, accentuates what Americans have in common and our positive evolution as a diverse society. By the 1980s, large segments of the educated American public accepted cultural pluralism. By contrast, the second vision of multiculturalism, which we have labeled "critical separatism," stresses cultural and ethnic differences and the nation's failure to live up to its ideals. In this essay, we argue for the first version of multiculturalism.

Note at the onset, however, that most of the leading multicultural theorists within social studies favor the critical separatist version. Such people write textbooks for the multicultural education courses that the large majority of pre- and in-service teachers are required to take. They also exercise considerable national influence in the construction of social studies standards and textbooks. The National Council for Accreditation of Teacher Education (NCATE) lists "diversity," a synonym for multicultural education, as one of seven required standards that all schools or departments of education must meet before it will approve their programs. NCATE now collaborates with 46 states in ensuring that future teachers receive "diversity" education (NCATE, 2002). Although a "diversity" standard is, at one level, innocuous, the problem is that the large majority of education professors directly responsible for having future and practicing teachers meet the standards believe in the critical separatist version of multiculturalism.

This poses a large problem for social studies. There are compelling reasons for social studies teachers to reject critical separatist multiculturalism because it is misleading, attacks ideals integral to American success, fosters ethnic discord, promotes extreme relativism, and is objectionable on educational, evidentiary, and political grounds. In this essay, we provide readers with what we believe to be an accurate and specific description of the worldviews and assertions of leading multiculturalists in American colleges and departments of education. We then analyze those ideas of the multiculturalists and offer alternatives that we believe to be more positive for both teachers and students.

THE THEORISTS' POLITICAL
AND PEDAGOGICAL PERSPECTIVES

We define as "theorists" those leaders of social studies education and other fields who are multicultural specialists and often cited in leading multicultural and social studies education journals. Virtually all multicultural theorists (hereinafter theorists) are education professors, and many specialize in social studies. In two seminal articles, J.S. Leming (1989, 1992) concluded that, as a group, leading social studies education professors were politically to the left of social studies teachers, all teachers, all professors, and the general public. In Leming's words, "Social studies theorists tend to see society in crisis, the dream unfulfilled, and the need for major changes to be brought about by greater citizen participation. Teachers tend to hold a less alarmist point of view and wish to preserve traditional values and practices" (1989, p. 407). Leming was so impressed by the political and philosophical differences between leading social studies professionals and other educators that he used the phrase "two cultures" in the titles of both articles (1989, p. 404).

Multicultural theorists evince an even more negative view of American society than other members of the social studies professoriate. They identify unjust relations as causes of America's evils and see multicultural education as an agent for positive change (Banks, 1995a). Their discussions of U.S. ethnic relations are usually limited to the "racism" that "the European-American power structure creates to serve its own purpose. . ." (Pang, Gay, and Stanley, 1995, p. 312).

Theorists constantly focus upon the racism of the dominant (white) majority toward all other ethnic groups while ignoring racism's universality. One theorist, in comparing the plight of poor African children and the general position of U.S. black children, writes, "Moreover, while a child in an African country experiences the effects of poverty, he or she does not experience the stigma of past dehumanization and second-class citizenship and the modern realities of ghettoization and denial of opportunity that confront Americans of African descent" (Ukpokodu, 1999, p. 8). Some theorists even advocate abolishing any reference to the "white race" because of the insidious motives of the dominant white majority. Speaking at the 2000 annual meeting of the American Educational Research Association, one prominent multiculturalist had this to say: "If white educators wish to transform themselves into agents of social justice (and we would encourage them to do so), then we suggest that they accomplish this as Polish, Irish, Canadian, English, or French, etc., and not by identifying themselves with the vile historical fiction known as the white race" (McLaren and Farahmandpur, 2001, p. 74)

Theorists regularly argue that "whiteness" warps the perceptions of members of the "dominant majority culture," whether they are children, educators, or university students. The author of an article included in a popular annual compilation of multicultural pieces meant for pre- and in-service teachers describes the majority of white students as follows: "Most white children have spent their academic lives looking into distorted mirrors of their history and culture which only reflected people like themselves." In contrast, the author contends, "Most children of color have been pointed toward a narrow window, which offered an obstructed view of the world and their place in it" (Ukpokudu, 1999, p. 8).

The theorists' negative views of the dominant "European-American majority" apparently include many of the pre- and in-service teachers they instruct. The unrealistic and biased perceptions of "European-American" education majors and teachers about minorities and their lack of enthusiasm for multiculturalism are common topics in the theorists' literature. The strong resistance of many undergraduate and graduate education students to multicultural education requirements is also frequently addressed in theorists' academic journal articles. At one university, 24 multicultural education instructors identified as two of their greatest challenges student resistance and anger displayed toward multicultural topics and opposition and hostility toward multicultural education instructors for promoting the examination of concepts such as tolerance and acceptance (Gallavan, 2000). How much of the alleged student resistance to multicultural education is a result of negative reactions to instructors' distorted portraits of a deeply racist America is a question the theorists do not explore.

The theorists' negative views of white teachers (and future teachers) are best illustrated in the concept of "white privilege" and its attendant literature. "White privilege" is defined as according benefits to whites on a purely ascriptive basis—their race, as opposed to their merit. In an interview published in *Rethinking Schools*, Christine Sleeter, a leading theorist and author of a substantial body of multicultural materials for education students, said this about white privilege: "Generally, people of European descent still claim white privileges. This is particularly true of wealthy people of European descent" (para. 2). Earlier in the same interview, she made clear that white privilege has, in her opinion, been an unchanging constant in the United States. In Sleeter's words:

> Both historically and in contemporary society, the relationships between racial and ethnic groups in this country are framed within a context of unequal power. People of European descent generally assume the power to claim the land, claim the resources, and claim the language. They even claim the right to frame the culture and identity of who we are as Americans. This has been the case ever since Columbus landed on the North American continent (Miner and Peterson, 2000-2001, para. 1).

Since their perspectives are grounded in this notion of permanent privilege of whites, for most theorists the goal of multiculturalism is not teaching a true appreciation for diversity. The stakes are higher. The central issue in multicultural education, for Sleeter and her fellow theorists, is a type of "justice" in which schools would advocate the reconstruction of society by transforming power relationships and redressing past grievances through various compensatory measures. In their view, teachers should begin promoting this goal in kindergarten. In the interview cited above, Sleeter recounts correcting a kindergarten teacher who had designed a lesson around Thanksgiving as a tool for teaching young children about the cultures of indigenous people.

> But that isn't the story. From the perspective of indigenous people, the real story has been one of genocide and of taking land away. It's important for kids to understand that story. From the perspective of indigenous people today, what's important is reclaiming land, reclaiming sover-

eignty, rebuilding economies, reclaiming and rebuilding cultures that have been devastated (Miner and Peterson, 2000-2001, para. 16).

Note the last sentence. Such theorists are not content simply to advocate teaching about treatment of Native-Americans and blacks from a historical perspective. They advocate using the public school classroom as a forum to promote the notion that there must be redress *now* for injustices that whites perpetrated, in some cases, centuries ago against people of color. A classroom focus upon content-based history education is, in the minds of the theorists, woefully inadequate. Instead, promotion of an activist agenda should be a major pedagogical goal, beginning in preschool. Since most multicultural theorists are educating for justice and activism, simply teaching about white racism is inadequate because it fails to demand compensatory action and the renegotiating of power relationships.

In addition to taking the "European-American power structure" to task for perpetuating racism, the theorists are also extremely critical of other traditional American values, particularly individualism, capitalism, and definitions of knowledge. In a 1995 article in *Theory and Research in Social Education*, three leading theorists identified individualism as a major "European-American" value perpetuated through the education system. They asserted that "past emphasis on individual competitiveness has caused a few to do exceptionally well while many others are plagued by powerlessness, oppression, economic hardships, and alienation" (Pang, Gay, and Stanley 1995, p. 322). In another article discussing critiques of multicultural education, a theorist described the attacks as "mainly about trying to maintain European and American capitalist supremacy" (Sleeter, 1995, p. 88).

Leading theorists are also strongly committed to postmodernism and its contention that knowledge is not neutral but reflects power relationships within society. In other words, school curricula foster the interests of the hegemonic elite. Sympathetic reviewers of *The Handbook of Research on Multicultural Education* (Banks and Banks, 1995a) identified the postmodernist definition of knowledge as central to the field. "A multicultural canon challenges the notion that knowledge represents verifiable truths" (Boyle-Baise, 1995, p. 335). Instead, the theorists view knowledge as a social construction defined by the dominant group. They seek to redefine knowledge in ways that present plural versions of the truth. In numerous articles, leading multicultural theorist James Banks has tried to refute notions of objective knowledge and universal rules of inquiry (1993; 1995b).

Because theorists promote the notion that objective truth is impossible, it is not surprising that they either find fault with knowledge transmission for its own sake or as a means to educate students to enter the work force or social structure. Such education is viewed as assimilationist and as creating problems for people of color (Banks, 1990, p. 211). The social studies content that the theorists promote seems to focus largely on teaching young people about ethnic groups other than those that are European. In *The Handbook of Research on Multicultural Education* (Banks and Banks, 1995a), the only nonethnic social studies content objective that the theorists recommended is a general commitment to America's unrealized democratic ideals.

The theorists are not interested in students learning a body of knowledge about different ethnic groups. Instead, their objective is to change student attitudes about themselves and others. They place a high priority on multicultural education as a tool to improve ethnic group relations, raise specific groups' self-esteem, and stimulate citizen action to transform America. In the words of a leading theorist, "multicultural education can be perceived as a pedagogy of the oppressed, resistance, hope, possibility, equity, emancipation, and reconstruction" (Gay, 1995, p. 5). The same writer asserts that a central theme of most theoretical conceptions of multiculturalism "is its potential for revolutionizing education, and ultimately, revitalizing society" (p. 38). The only way to accomplish education for citizenship in a multicultural society is through a transformation (of the schools) "as far reaching as the one that has seized Eastern Europe and what was once the Soviet Union" (Pang et al., 1995, p. 323).

Although readers might suppose that such rhetoric is a product of the political radicalism of the 1960s, this is not its sole source. Leading multiculturalists, in most respects, reiterate the Progressive philosophy of Social Reconstructionism. Long before the Vietnam War, Social Reconstructionists believed that schools and teachers should act as agents in effecting deliberate social change. Two contemporary multicultural theorists correctly define Social Reconstructionism as an approach that "directly challenges students to become social reformers and commit to the reconstruction of society through the redistribution of power and other resources" (Jenks, Lee, and Kanpol, 2002, p. 23). This framework encompasses the overarching belief that multicultural educators should seek to change power relations in order to effect a more just and equitable society. According to this view, education has traditionally been a tool of the hegemonic elite to retain the status quo with its highly inequitable power relations.

Although contemporary theorists often accentuate the connection between "European-American" elites and the disempowered, their assertions about what social studies teachers should teach to remedy America's ills have roots at least 70 years deep. In his 1932 book, *Dare the Schools Build a New Social Order?*, prominent progressive George Counts, who founded Social Reconstructionism, advocated the elimination of capitalism, competition, property rights, and profits. Counts emphasized that schools should be the vanguard of America's political, economic, and social transformation (Ravitch, 2000). Contemporary theorists echo Counts' indictment of capitalism, individualism, and competition. They also reiterate his emphasis on schools as training centers for social activism instead of institutions that focus primarily upon the transmission of knowledge.

APPRAISING THE THEORISTS

The notion that "European-American" elements of our society continue to be racist relative to other ethnic groups runs contrary to recent historical and contemporary evidence. Glazer (1997, p. 46) accurately summarized the historical case against the theorists when he asserted that, if one examines recent American history, one finds greater inclusion, a steady increase in constitutional and legal protection for minorities, and an abandonment of racial restrictions in U.S. immigration law. In his critically acclaimed book, *Bowling Alone* (2000), Robert Putnam cites a number of studies indicating "without a doubt, America in the 1990s was a more tolerant place than America in the 1950s or even the 1970s" (p. 352).

In *America in Black and White: One Nation Indivisible, Race in Modern America* (1997), social scientists Stephan and Abigail Thernstrom provided even more impressive evidence of increases in the legal rights and educational progress of blacks, who, until 2003, comprised the largest American minority group. The authors used the early 1940s as a beginning point and concluded their work with the mid-1990s. They chronicle the end of "separate but equal" and the passage of the voting and civil rights acts. In part because American democracy worked and government-supported racism ended, blacks have made substantial educational and economic progress. In 1960, 20 percent of the black population completed four or more years of high school. By 1995 that figure had risen to approximately 74 percent (p. 190). In 1960, 7 percent of blacks attended and only 3 percent graduated from college. By 1995, these figures were 38 percent and 13 percent (p. 192). In 1940, black male median income was 41 percent that of white males and black female income 36 percent that of white females. By 1995, the median income percentage for black males relative to whites had risen to 67 percent, while black female median income had soared to 89 percent of white female median income (p. 195). Over three times as many blacks in 1995 (41 percent) identified themselves as middle class than the 12 percent who did so in 1949 (p. 200). The authors convincingly document that the educational attainment deficit of blacks relative to whites, not direct white racism, accounts for most remaining economic gaps. Although no scholars have marshaled the massive amount of evidence depicting the progress of other ethnic groups to the degree that the Thernstroms have in the case of blacks, the end of legal racial segregation and the passage of civil rights laws have resulted in dramatic educational and economic advances for all U.S. ethnic minorities over the past half century.

An examination of the materials that social studies multiculturalists use with their pre- and in-service captive student audiences indicates that they simply do not include this kind of accurate historical content, thereby grossly distorting the last 60 years of American history. Through these distortions, they perpetuate the notion of "white guilt" when there is no reason in the 21st century for the vast majority of whites to feel guilty about issues of ethnicity.

Multicultural theorists further mislead students and distort reality by never focusing upon the international comparative data on how majority populations in other countries feel about their principal minorities. In one 1991 study comparing the United States to 12 European countries, random samples of Europeans and American majority populations were asked if they disliked their nations' principal minorities. For example, 42 percent of the French sample disliked North Africans, and the same percentage of Poles disliked Ukrainians. The U.S. ranked lowest of all 13 countries in the percentage of majority citizens (13) who held unfavorable attitudes toward blacks, who, at the time, comprised the largest minority group in the U.S. (Thernstrom and Thernstrom, p. 531). When such evidence is objectively examined, it strongly supports the argument that the United States has, by world standards, evolved into a society that is highly tolerant of ethnic minorities. Multicultural theorists, with their stubborn insistence that we are deeply flawed by our racism, prefer to ignore such comparisons.

The theorists' attack upon the "European-American" values of individualism and capitalism neglects the positive influence of both those values in the battle against racism. Western beliefs in individual rights and liberty formed the foundation of the American civil rights movement. Despite its flaws, the capitalist/competitive aspect of American society, far from causing the few to prosper at everyone else's expense, has resulted in extremely high levels of affluence for the majority of Americans by world standards and is a major reason why enormous numbers of foreigners desire to live here.

The theorists' postmodern perspective poses a serious challenge to the idea that what is taught in history and the social sciences can be based upon evidence. If there are always "multiple truths," then what is taught as content becomes simply a matter of competing opinions. In recent years, the anti-intellectual implications of postmodernism have been a major topic of criticism by academics on the Left and Right, and there is even some evidence that postmodernism is becoming passé in the academy (Sweezy et al., 1995). Yet none of the controversy over its negative, nihilistic, and relativistic implications is present in the writings of social studies theorists.

To the contrary, their writings are, if anything, extremely relativistic regarding every conceivable cultural and minority group except so-called "European-Americans," where they usually take an absolute stance of negativity. Many hold the opinion that the values and norms of the various subcultures within a society should be equally protected by law and sanctified by and celebrated in curricula. In other words, the multiplicity of values and norms should be uncritically enshrined in the classroom. But as the late Albert Shanker (1996) cautioned:

> The claims of multiculturalists and other separatists reflect the attitude that no one group may make a judgment on any other, since all "depends on your point of view." This extremely relativistic viewpoint conflicts with the need that all societies have of establishing some basic values, guidelines, and beliefs. And, it should be pointed out that those who reject this claim are ironically making an absolute value of tolerance, for in its name they are unwilling to make any other value judgment (para. 13).

Taken to its logical extreme, the theorists' refusal to make cultural value judgments would have us teaching tolerance of any number of practices repugnant to most Americans, such as female genital mutilation (practiced in 28 countries in the Middle East and sub-Saharan Africa), immolation of Hindu widows on their husbands' funeral pyres, amputations as punishments for theft, ethnic cleansing, and attacking innocent people in the Pentagon and the World Trade Center to avenge alleged grievances.

The theorists' focus on emphasizing ethnic differences as a means of empowering young people of color is not supported by evidence. It is also potentially dangerous to the fabric of American society.

Theorists contend that multicultural education improves interethnic relations and minority self-esteem, thereby improving academic performance. But they cite little evidence. In *The Handbook of Research on Multicultural Education*, several theorists themselves acknowledged the paucity of studies that support the effectiveness of educational interventions designed to improve intergroup attitudes. The notion that an ethnic group's self esteem and subsequent academic achievement can improve through the study of its own culture has almost no supporting evidence. In fact, the counterevidence is strong. It is well known that American students think better of their own performance in mathematics than do Chinese, Japanese, or Korean students, even as Asians objectively do better. Within the United States, the achievements of Asians and Jews, who had no multiculturalism designed to make them feel better about being Asian or Jewish, are well documented; blacks, who on average have lower levels of academic achievement than other ethnic groups, generally show up in research as having higher self-esteem than other groups (Glazer, 1997, p. 54).

The divisive results for American society of a multicultural education that dwells on the injustices whites have committed toward ethnic minorities and ignores the substantial evidence of improvement in U.S. relations should not be taken lightly. Glazer, a Harvard emeritus professor of sociology and education, illustrated the point well when he wrote:

What would be better for young blacks to believe: That everyone is against them? That all their protections are shams? That whites will always stop them from getting ahead? That their oppression has been scarcely reduced since the days before the civil rights revolution and the Civil Rights Act? Or would it be better for them to believe the reverse: That the vast majority of Americans wish them well? That their civil rights are protected by the laws of the land? That their historic oppression at the hand of citizens and law enforcement officials is slowly but steadily declining? (Glazer, 1997, p. 47).

What is tragic is that most multicultural theorists waste scarce pre- and in-service teacher time by completely ignoring legitimate educational problems related to ethnicity. The outstanding case in point is the grave academic problem faced by many blacks and Hispanics in the United States.

It has been widely documented by such scholars as Jenks and Phillips (1998), Abigail Thernstrom (2002), and Ornstein and Levine (2003) that a significant academic achievement gap exists between blacks and Hispanics on the one hand and their Asian and white peers on the other. In both reading and math, on average, blacks and Hispanics who are high school seniors perform about as well as white and Asian freshmen on standardized tests.

If blacks and Hispanics are to realize substantial educational and economic improvement, this problem must be solved. Making future and practicing teachers aware of the academic achievement gap and assisting them in devising ways to narrow it should be a major agenda item in every department and college of education in the U.S. The strategies that successful schools serving minorities have employed to reduce the achievement gap by raising math and reading scores should constitute primary multicultural course content in the training of teachers. However, because of the Social Reconstructionist leanings of the theorists, this serious problem is not being addressed because it remains invisible to most education majors and teachers.

A survey of a widely used multicultural reader intended for future teachers indicated that not one of the 37 articles in the publication included a discussion of the achievement gap (Schultz, 2003). Although the typical student in a multicultural class is inundated with materials about European-American racism, "white privilege," and the particular educational needs of every conceivable ethnic and cultural group, including Gypsies, the racial-ethnic achievement gap is an invisible issue in multicultural courses.

Not only do multicultural theorists fail to prepare teachers to deal with such bona fide educational concerns, their insistence that American society should be radically transformed and that public school students must be trained to be change agents is a waste of public monies and, arguably, a violation of the public trust. There is no evidence that the vast majority of Americans concur with the theorists' perceptions of the United States or are even aware of the radical nature of much multicultural content that future teachers are required to study.

Although conservatives traditionally have worried about the potential impact of radical multiculturalism upon the fabric of American society, Glazer, a political moderate, is only one of several distinguished nonconservative academics who seriously challenge the extremism of separatist multiculturalism. Pulitzer Prize-winning historian Arthur Schlesinger (1998) incurred the wrath of the theorists when, in a book on multiculturalism, he identified assimilation as our greatest achievement. "The genius of America," Schlesinger wrote, "lies in its capacity to forge a single nation from peoples of remarkably diverse racial, religious, and ethnic origins" (p. 142). Political liberal E.D. Hirsch Jr. who, through the Core Knowledge movement, promotes greater curricular and social cohesion for all students, has also been pilloried by the theorists. One reviewer of his book, writing in the *Harvard Educational Review*, accused Hirsch of posing ". . . serious threats to a social order already unjust and unequal" (Buras, 1999, p. 91). Apparently the theorists who attack Hirsch completely ignore the substantial content on ethnic minorities to be found in the Core Knowledge Curricular Sequence that is utilized by elementary schools (Core Knowledge Foundation, 1999).

While September 11 caused many thoughtful Americans to wonder if more should be done in our schools to renew a sense of national identity and strengthen social cohesion, the theorists did not tone down their rhetoric. They even urged students to search for explanations as to what the U.S. had done to deserve such retaliatory acts of terrorism. The theorists asserted that still more multicultural education is necessary, since Americans seem not to "understand" the perspectives of the terrorists and the cultures and religions that spawn them.

MULTICULTURALISM ABROAD

Critical separatist multiculturalism is not exclusive to this country. Throughout the West and elsewhere, an entire cadre of intellectuals promotes a body of ideas that scholar John Fonte identifies as "Transnational Progressivism" (Fonte, 2002). They contend that group rights transcend those of the individual, that all societies have oppressor and victim groups, and that national symbols, narratives, and the very idea of national citizenship should be eradicated in order for human society to evolve. There is mounting evidence from abroad that any country in which separatist multiculturalism becomes influential will encounter the kinds of social discord that now threaten us. Like Fonte, Stephen Heyneman (2001, p. 6) has also studied social cohesion and argues that schooling should "provide a common underpinning for citizenship." He asserts that the purpose of education should be to develop social capital and foster nation building.

Eaton (2002) recently studied the development of the highly multicultural curricula that have taken root in some of the Russian Federation republics during the past decade. The development of multicultural curricula at the local and regional levels was viewed by proponents, including many Western think tanks, government agencies, and nonprofits, as giving voice to groups that had been marginalized or ignored in the former, Russocentric curriculum of the USSR. But Eaton found that the extreme multiculturalism that has developed in some of the wealthier, "sovereignty-minded" republics in particular, has resulted in curricula that foster hyper-pluralism, interethnic tensions, religious conflict, and center (Moscow)-periphery clashes.

Separatist multicultural ideas put into practice in Great Britain have contributed to fragmentation and violent conflict in that country. The Labor Party's far-left wing, supported by black nationalists and radical political groups, has succeeded in instituting multicultural policies over the past two decades (Hyland, 2001). In well-intentioned efforts to respect cultural differences in the pluralistic city of Bradford, the Bradford Council implemented such policies top-down in an attempt to diffuse racial and cultural tension. To say that these policies boomeranged is an understatement.

The premise underpinning these policies was that "every section of the community 'had an equal right to maintain its own identity, culture, language, religion and customs'" (Malik, 2001, Multiculturalism transformed, para. 4). The Bradford Council proceeded to meet demands for Muslim-only schools, for separate education for girls, and for funding various religious and cultural groups' projects. The Labor Party sanctioned and subsidized faith-based religious education in state schools. Authors of a 2001 report on the Bradford situation found "63 supplementary schools for Muslim children in Bradford, five Hindu schools, six Sikh schools and five Eastern and Western European schools" (Hyland, 2001, para. 22).

Increasingly, these culturally and racially based groups engaged in bitter competition to increase their shares of government subventions, pitting one group against another and further fragmenting the community. The community became polarized and consumed by tension that erupted into violent riots, which then prompted a review of Bradford's multicultural policies (Hyland, 2001). It found that "multiculturalism has helped segregate communities far more effectively than racism. It has not simply entrenched the divisions created by racism, but made cross-cultural interaction more difficult by encouraging people to assert their cultural differences" (Malik, 2001, in Bradford, Multiculturalism, para. 6). "It also contributed to a system of educational apartheid in the state sector, in which schools are increasingly 'monocultural,' either all white or all Asian" (Hyland, 2001).

One might reason that Britain's inclusive multicultural policies would foster greater identification with the nation, since the varied curricula would give voice to diverse elements within the society that had previously felt excluded or marginalized. However, a well-publicized survey by an Asian radio station of 500 Muslims in Greater London indicated that 98 percent would not fight for Britain while 48 percent would fight for Osama bin Laden or Islam (Appleton, 2001). The "community of communities" policies, which foster and endorse enclaves of separate groups with their own particular identities within the larger polity, have had the effect of destroying any sense of allegiance beyond the various separate "communities," thus corroding community and national cohesion.

Great Britain and the Russian Federation are not the only examples of the dangers of excessive multiculturalism. Hyperpluralism and tribalization have well-established histories of shattering nation-states, as has been evidenced recently in the Balkans and more than a few African countries. Given the realities of today's world, the potential balkanization of America via extreme multicultural approaches to education is not the answer for solving the remaining problems perceived by groups within our society.

If 9/11 taught us anything, it should have been the value of national unity within a democratic framework in confronting the daunting challenges of terrorism and fanaticism. Such unity comes from continually holding in mind that teaching our common culture is a paramount educational goal.

MULTICULTURALISM BASED ON THE EVIDENCE

Historian Diane Ravitch (1990) aptly described the role of multiculturalism in American schools when she wrote, "Paradoxical though it may seem, the United States has a common culture that is multicultural" (p. 339). In social studies, it is essential that youth learn specific information about the common political ideals and institutions that make us American and, at the same time, learn specific content about the different cultural and ethnic groups that live in our nation. Classicist Mary Lefkowitz (1996), in reference to a question about what constitutes appropriate classroom content, asserted, "When it comes to deciding what one can or cannot say in class, the question of ethnicity or of motivation, whether personal or cultural, is or ought to be irrelevant. What matters is whether what one says is supported by facts and evidence, tests or formulae" (p. 162). Social studies teachers who select multicultural content based on evidence are more likely to transmit accurate information to students than teachers who view the class, race, or gender of authors as more important than the quality of their works. When social studies educators make the criterion of evidence-based content paramount in selecting multicultural materials, then the danger is minimized that ideological goals will distort the educational process.

Before the 1960s, the dominant message in school history and social studies was that white males were exclusively responsible for the development of the United States, and depictions of people of color and women contained serious flaws. As a nation, we have come a long way from the racism and sexism that underpinned "white male" American history. It is very important that social studies teachers develop high quality multicultural education programs. The best way to achieve this goal is to base multicultural education on evidence and sound scholarship, instead of the ideological and affective perspectives that the theorists espouse.

RECOMMENDATIONS

First, teachers should develop American history courses that fairly describe the experiences and contributions of minority groups. Accurate U.S. history instruction will send the message that, as a nation, we are now one of the world's most advanced societies in treatment of minority groups. In part due to this positive development, teachers can and should draw upon a multicultural pantheon of people of color who have realized the American dream. No heterogeneous society has entirely harmonious relations among its ethnic and cultural groups. However, in their attempt to correct for past neglect of minorities in U.S. history courses, multicultural theorists have distorted and even suppressed the truth about America's progress in race relations and successes of people of color. The perpetration of these inaccuracies must end.

Second, social studies instructors at all levels should reject the theorists' notion that all cultures are equal; that fanaticism, terrorism, and inhumanity should be tolerated if they can be rationalized; and that we have no right to criticize and condemn evil. This can be most effectively done by the development of content-oriented world history, geography, and cultures courses. If these are well taught, students will learn numerous instances of good and evil in the human experience and have opportunities to compare and contrast cultural practices.

Third, educators should teach about unity in the United States, as well as disunity, about our accomplishments as well as our blemishes, and about the value of working together as a whole to achieve common objectives. We should also teach students to take pride in the achievements and progress of the nation since its inception. Building a sense of reasoned patriotism is an integral part of creating social cohesion, identification with the nation, and a civil society. This does not mean that we should teach or preach blind nationalism, ethnocentrism, or jingoism. But all societies use education as a means of inculcating patriotic values; this is the socialization process. The danger in placing the locus of American identity in its separate minorities, rather than in the nation as the unifying unit, is tribalization, the balkanization of our country at a time when greater cohesion is needed to confront the challenges to both our way of life and global security.

Fourth, teachers should not assume the role of social activists who dwell upon the negatives in our society and urge students to struggle against various oppressors. Rather, our students should be taught to develop their own interpretations and analyses of history and culture after becoming thoroughly grounded in evidence-based studies that do not represent the views of one ideologue or another. Likewise, they should develop, through the study of American government and politics, a thorough understanding of how to effect needed changes through democratic processes.

Finally, teachers should reject the theorists and demand content-based multicultural teaching materials. Policy makers and the general public must be made fully aware that radical leftist multicultural ideas have been institutionalized in teacher education programs through such things as NCATE requirements that compel the nation's future teachers to learn distortions of reality that are antithetical to what most Americans believe. We believe that once policy makers and the larger public are fully informed that their tax dollars actually support the inculcation of radical multicultural notions in future and practicing history and social studies teachers, the stage will be set for changing those requirements.

NOTE

1. A shorter version of this essay was published in *Social Studies*, March-April 1998, 89(2), 57-60.

REFERENCES

Appleton, J. (2001, November 5). Value-free Britain. Retrieved on November 29, 2002, from the Spiked Politics website: http://www.spikedonline.com/Articles/00000002D2AC.htm.

Banks. J.A. (1990). Citizenship education for a pluralistic democratic society. *The Social Studies,* 81(5), 210-14.

Banks, J.A. (1993). Multicultural education: Development, dimensions, and challenges. *Phi Delta Kappan,* 75(1), 22-28.

Banks, J.A., and Banks, C.A.M. (Eds.). (1995a). *The handbook of research on multicultural education.* New York: Macmillan.

Banks, J.A. (1995b). Multicultural education: Historical development, dimensions, practice. In J.A. Banks and C.A.M. Banks (Eds.). *The handbook of research on multicultural education.* New York: Macmillan.

Banks, J.A. (1995c). Multicultural education: Its effects on students' racial and gender role attitudes. In J.A. Banks and C.A.M. Banks (Eds.). *The handbook of research on multicultural education,* New York: Macmillan.

Banks, J.A. (1995d). The transformative challenges to the social science disciplines: Implications for social studies teaching and learning. *Theory and Research in Social Education,* 23(1), 2-33.

Bay, G. (1997). The relationship between multicultural and democratic education. *The Social Studies,* 88 (1), 5-11.

Boyle-Baise, M. (1995). The role of a European American scholar in multicultural education. *Theory and Research in Social Education,* 23(4), 342-54.

Bradford's race divisions condemned. (2001, July 16). Retrieved on November 28, 2002 from the British Broadcasting Website:

http://news.bbc.co.uk/1/hi/uk/1435062.stm

Buras, K. (1999, November 1). Questioning core assumptions: A critical reading of and response to E. D. Hirsch's *The schools we need and why we don't have the*m. *Harvard Educational Review, 69*, 67-93.

Core Knowledge Foundation. (1999). *Core knowledge sequence: Content guidelines for grades K-8.* Charlottesville, VA: Core Knowledge Foundation.

De Bary, T. (1995). Multiculturalism, civility, and human rights (part 11). *Freedom Review*, 26(3), 41-46.

Eaton, J. (2002). *Curricular decentralization in four Russian Federation Republics: A sociopolitical analysis.* Unpublished doctoral dissertation; Widener University; Chester, PA.

Fonte, J. (2002, Spring). Ideological war within the West. *Orbis*, 46(3), 449-467.

Gallavan, N.P. (2000). Multicultural education at the academy: Teacher educators' challenges, conflicts, and coping skills. In F. Schultz (Ed.); *Multicultural Education: Annual Edition*, 2002-2003. Guilford, CT: McGraw-Hill/Dushkin. (Reprinted from *Equity and Excellence in Education*. [Dec] 5-11.)

Gay, G. (1995). Curriculum theory and multicultural education. In J.A. Banks and C.A.M. Banks (Eds.) *The handbook of research on multicultural education.* New York: Macmillan.

Glazer, N. (1997). *We are all multiculturalists now.* Cambridge: Harvard University Press.

Heyneman, S.P. (1999). Development aid in education: A personal view. *International Journal of Educational Development*, 19(3), 183-190.

Heyneman, S.P. (2001). *Education and social cohesion.* Manuscript submitted for publication.

Hyland, J. (2001, July 24). Britain: Bradford report shows dead end of racially-based politics. Retrieved on November 28, 2002, from World Socialist website: http://www.wsws.org/articles/

2001/jul2001/brad-j24.shtml.

Jenks, C., Lee, J.O., and Kanpol, B. (2002). Approaches to multicultural education in pre-service teacher education: Philosophical frameworks and models for teaching. In F. Schultz (Ed.), *Multicultural education: Annual edition, 2002-2003*. Guilford, CT: McGraw-Hill/Dushkin. (Reprinted from *The Urban Review*, 33[2], 87-105.)

Jenks, C., and Phillips, M. (Eds.) (1998). *The black-white test score gap*. Washington, DC: Brookings Institution.

Lefkowitz, M. (1996). *Not out of Africa: How Afrocentrism became an excuse to teach myth as history*. New York: Basic Books.

Leming, J.S. (1989). The two cultures of social studies education. *Social Education*, 53(6), 404-08.

Leming, J.S. (1992). Ideological perspectives within the social studies profession: An empirical examination of the two cultures thesis. *Theory and Research in Social Education*, 20(3), 293-312.

Malik, K. (2001, December). The trouble with multiculturalism. Retrieved on November 28, 2002 from the Spiked Politics web pages: http://www.spiked-online.com/articles/00000002D35E.htm

Miner, B. and Peterson, B. (2000-2001). Diversity vs. white privilege: An interview with Christine Sleeter. *Rethinking schools: An urban educational journal*, 15(2). Retrieved January 5, 2001, from http://www.rethinkingschools.org/Archives/15_02/Int152.htm.

McLaren, P. and Farahmandpur, R., (2001). Class, cultism, and multiculturalism: A notebook on forging a revolutionary politics. In F. Schultz (Ed.). *Multicultural education: Annual edition, 2002-2003*. Guilford, CT: McGraw-Hill/Dushkin. (Reprinted from *Multicultural Education*, Spring, 5-11.)

National Council for Accreditation of Teacher Education. (2002). Professional Standards for the Accreditation of Schools, Colleges, and Departments of Education. Washington, DC: National Council for the Accreditation of Teacher Education.

Ornstein, A. and Levine, D. (2003). *Foundations of education* (8th edition). Boston: Houghton Mifflin.

Pang, V. O., and Park, C. (1992). Issues-centered approaches to multicultural education in the middle grades. *The Social Studies,* 83(3), 108-12.

Pang, V. O., Gay, G., and Stanley, W. B. (1995). Expanding conceptions of community and civic competence for a multicultural society. *Theory and Research in Social Education,* 23(4), 302-27.

Putnam, R.D. (2000). *Bowling alone: The collapse and revival of American community.* New York: Simon and Schuster.

Ravitch, D. (1990). Multiculturalism: E pluribus plures. *The American Scholar,* 59(3), 337-54.

Ravitch, D. (2000). *Left back: A century of failed school reforms.* Simon and Schuster: New York.

Schlesinger, A.M., Jr. (1998 ed.). *The disuniting of America: Reflections on a multicultural society.* New York: W. W. Norton.

Schultz, F. (Ed.). (2001). *Multicultural education: Annual edition, 2001-2002.* Guilford, CT: McGraw-Hill/Dushkin.

Schultz, F. (Ed.). (2002). *Multicultural education: Annual edition, 2002-2003.* Guilford, CT: McGraw-Hill/Dushkin.

Schultz, F. (Ed.). (2003). *Multicultural education: Annual edition, 2003-2004.* Guilford, CT: McGraw-Hill/Dushkin.

Shanker, A. (1996, July). The importance of civic education. *Issues in Democracy,* 1(8). Retrieved September 10, 2002, from USIA Electronic Journals at http://usinfo.state.gov/journals/itdhr/0796/ijde/shanker.htm.

Sleeter, C. (1995). An analysis of the critiques of multicultural education. In J.A. Banks and C.A.M. Banks (Eds.). *The handbook of research on multicultural education.* New York: Macmillan.

Sweezy, P.M., Magdoff, H., and Huberman, L. (Eds.). Wood, E.M. and Foster, J.B. (guest eds.). (1995). In defense of history. *Monthly Review,* 47(3), 1-157.

Thernstrom, A. (2002). The racial gap in academic achievement. In A. Thernstrom and S. Thernstrom (Eds.). *Beyond the color line: New perspectives on race and ethnicity in America.* Palo Alto, CA: Hoover Institution.

Thernstrom, S. and Thernstrom, A. (1997). *America in Black and White: One Nation, Indivisible.* New York: Simon and Schuster.

Ukpokodu, N. (1999). Multiculturalism vs. Globalism. In F. Schultz (Ed.), *Multicultural Education: Annual Edition, 2002-2003.* Guilford, CT: McGraw-Hill/Dushkin. (Reprinted from *Social Education,* [September 1999], p. 298-300.)

5

Teacher-Centered Instruction
The Rodney Dangerfield of Social Studies

Mark C. Schug

During the 1970s and 1980s, a line of educational research developed called "effective teaching." Effective teachers were reported to favor research-supported practices that, when properly implemented in the classroom, produced stronger academic achievement.

The name given to such instruction has varied. Terms like "active teaching" and "explicit instruction" were used from time to time. Such phrases conveyed the image of teachers on their feet in the front of the room with eyes open, asking questions, making points, gesturing, writing key ideas on the board, encouraging, correcting, demonstrating, and so forth. The role of the teacher was obvious and explicit and tied to clearly identified content or skills.

For the purposes of this paper, I use the term "teacher-centered instruction" to refer to this approach. It implies a high degree of teacher direction and a focus of students on academic tasks. And it vividly contrasts with student-centered or constructivist approaches in establishing a leadership role for the teacher. Teacher presentation, demonstration, drill and practice, posing of numerous factual questions, and immediate feedback and correction are all key elements.

Teacher-centered instruction has again and again proven its value in studies that show it to be an especially effective instructional method. Yet, when self-appointed education leaders meet to share best practices or write about effective teaching, teacher-centered instruction, as the comedian Rodney Dangerfield used to say, gets no respect.

STUDENT-CENTERED INSTRUCTION

In fact, for most of the last century social studies leaders have fought hard against the idea of teacher-centered instruction. At nearly every opportunity— in journal articles, education textbooks, and speeches at professional meetings —slogans were voiced about teaching the child, not the subject, according to developmentally appropriate practices. Those who favor student-centered approaches suggest that:

- "Hands-on" activities are superior to teacher-led instruction. Projects, group work, field trips, almost any other approach is to be preferred.
- Integrated content is superior to discipline-specific content. The barriers between the disciplines such as history and geography are the artificial creations of self-serving academics. Integrated themes are regarded as having greater integrity.
- Cooperative, group-learning approaches are superior to whole group, teacher-led instruction. Students learn best by interacting with each other rather than by learning from adults.
- Academic content is inherently dull. Topics such as social issues have more relevance and appeal to students than subjects such as economics or geography.

Is there an alternative to student-centered instruction? If so, what research supports it and how does it look in practice? Let's examine the often-overlooked case for teacher-centered instruction.

RESEARCH ON TEACHER-CENTERED INSTRUCTION: DIRECT INSTRUCTION IN READING

Teacher-centered instruction derives from two lines of scholarship and curriculum development (Schug, Tarver, and Western, 2001). One is associated primarily with the work of Siegfried Engelmann and his colleagues, whose approach is widely referred to as "Direct Instruction" and whose research focused predominantly on reading. The other line of scholarship is associated primarily with the work of Barak Rosenshine and his colleagues, whose "process-outcome" research identified the teacher practices that were associated with improving student learning.

Engelmann's work derives from close analysis of the comprehension and reasoning skills needed for successful student performance in reading or mathematics, skills that provide the intellectual substance of the Direct Instruction programs he developed. In the case of reading, its substance is found in the sound system of spoken English and the ways in which English sounds are represented in writing—a major reason why Direct Instruction in reading is associated with phonemic awareness or phonics. But it is not equivalent to phonics. Direct Instruction can be used to teach things other than phonics—mathematics and social studies, for example—and phonics can be taught by means other than Direct Instruction.

The detailed character of the Direct Instruction approach developed by Englemann derives from a learning theory and a set of teaching practices linked to that theory. The learning theory focuses on how children generalize from present understanding to understanding new examples. This theory informs the sequencing of classroom tasks for children and the means by which teachers lead children through those tasks. The means include a complex system of scripted remarks, questions, and signals to which children provide individual and choral responses in extended, highly interactive sessions. Children in Direct Instruction classrooms also do written work in workbooks or on activity sheets.

An impressive body of research over 25 years attests to the efficacy of Engelmann's model. In the most comprehensive review, Adams and Engelmann (1996) identified 34 well-designed studies in which Direct Instruction interventions were compared to other teaching strategies. These studies reported 173 comparisons, spanning the years from 1972 to 1996. The comparison yielded two major results. First, 87 percent of posttreatment test score averages favored Direct Instruction, compared to 12 percent favoring other approaches. Second, 64 percent of the statistically significant outcomes favored Direct Instruction compared to only one percent favoring other approaches, and 35 percent favoring neither.

A meta-analysis of data from the 34 studies also yielded large effect sizes for Direct Instruction. Large gains were reported for both regular and special education students, for elementary and secondary students, and for achievement in a variety of subjects including reading, mathematics, spelling, health, and science. The average effect size for the 34 studies was .87; the average effect size calculated for the 173 comparisons was .97. This means that gain scores for students in Direct Instruction groups averaged nearly a full standard deviation above those of students in comparison groups. Effect sizes of this magnitude are rare in education research.

Teacher-Centered Instruction in Reading and Other Subjects

The second line of research in teacher-centered instruction is based on a synthesis of findings from experimental studies conducted by many different scholars working independently, mostly in the 1980s. In these studies, teachers were trained to use specific instructional practices. The effects of these practices on student learning were determined by comparing similar students' learning in classes where the practices were not used. The synthesis growing out of these studies identified common "teaching functions" that proved effective in improving student learning.

This research reached its zenith in 1986 when Rosenshine and Robert Stevens co-authored a chapter in the *Handbook of Research on Teaching*. The chapter reviewed several empirical studies that focused on key instructional behaviors of teachers. In several of the experiments, they found that effective teachers attended to inappropriate student behavior, maintained the attention of all students, provided immediate feedback and evaluation, set clear expectations, and engaged students as a group in learning. Rosenshine and Stevens (1986) distilled the research down to a set of behaviors that characterize well-structured lessons. Effective teachers, they said:

- Open lessons by reviewing prerequisite learning.

- Provide a short statement of goals.
- Present new material in small steps, with student practice after each step.
- Give clear and detailed instructions and explanations.
- Provide a high level of active practice for all students.
- Ask a large number of questions, check for understanding, and obtain responses from all students.
- Guide students during initial practice.
- Provide systematic feedback and corrections.
- Provide explicit instruction and practice for seatwork exercises and, where necessary, monitor students during seatwork.

The major components of this sort of teacher-centered instruction are not all that unexpected. All teachers use some of these behaviors some of the time, but the most effective teachers use most of them nearly all the time.

Interest in Rosenshine's second line of research was given an important boost from E.D. Hirsch, Jr.'s book, *The Schools We Need & Why We Don't Have Them* (1996). He summarized findings from several studies which contributed to the conclusion that teacher-centered instruction works well in classrooms.

The first was a series of "process-outcome" studies conducted from 1970 until 1973 at the University of Canterbury in New Zealand. They showed that time spent focused on content and the amounts of content taught were important factors in achievement. Whether a lecture or questioning format was used, careful structuring of content by the teacher followed by summary reviews was the most effective method.

In a later series of studies, Jere Brophy and his colleagues (1973-1979) found that some teachers got consistently good results while others did not. They observed the teachers associated with good and poor academic outcomes and reached at least two startling conclusions—first, that teachers who produced the least achievement used approaches that were more concerned with the students' self-esteem, and second, that learning progressed best when the materials were not only new and challenging but could also be easily grasped by students. Brophy and his colleagues also found that the most effective teachers were likely to:

- Maintain a sustained focus on content.
- Involve all students.
- Maintain a brisk pace.
- Teach skills to the point of overlearning.
- Provide immediate feedback.

Finally, in a separate series of process-outcome studies that spanned the period from the 1960s to the 1980s, Gage and his colleagues at Stanford University found that effective teachers:

- Introduce materials with an overview or analogy.
- Use review and repetition.
- Praise and repeat student answers.
- Give assignments that offer practice and variety.
- Ensure questions and assignments are new and challenging yet easy enough to allow success with reasonable effort.

TEACHER-CENTERED INSTRUCTION IN SOCIAL STUDIES

Though research on teacher-centered instruction focuses on the day-to-day work of teachers who favor this approach, the rhetoric of leaders in social studies education fails to take note of these highly successful teachers. A review of recent articles in *Theory and Research in Social Education*, the flagship research journal of the National Council for the Social Studies and the College and University Assembly, makes this point abundantly clear. The authors and editor emphasize issues of social justice, race, gender, and class, while failing to address what are the most *effective* teacher practices. Teachers who favor teacher-centered instruction are rarely the subjects of interviews or observation, and their teaching style and techniques are rarely mentioned. When such teachers are noticed at all by the leaders of the field, it is to use them as examples of what not to do in the classroom. After all, these teachers have rejected most of the hip, student-centered approaches. They are ignored or dismissed by the self-appointed leadership crowd—the folks who speak at professional meetings, write the textbooks for teachers, and dominate professional discussion. Again, Rodney Dangerfield's line might best describe such teachers. They get no respect!

There is some evidence that, despite the heavy emphasis placed on student-centered techniques, many social studies teachers might be successfully using teacher-centered instruction in the classroom. It is hard to be certain, however, because as Cuban (1991) observes, studies of classroom observations are rare in social studies. In his summary of the studies that are available, he concludes that the most common pattern of social studies teaching includes heavy emphasis on the teacher and the textbook as the sources of information for assignments and discussion, followed by tests and seatwork—in other words, teacher-centered instruction. Whole group instruction dominates. Cuban comments that this state of affairs seems nearly impervious to serious change. This observation is congruent with observations made by others of social studies classrooms (Goodlad, 1984). But, if this is so, is it as bad as Cuban implies?

Educators who use teacher-centered approaches are generally reluctant to use esoteric forms of instruction, and many effective teachers have not found success using student-centered teaching approaches. Consider cooperative learning as an example. Its research base is impressive in terms of its potential to achieve academic and social outcomes (Slavin, 1990). But in practice, this potential is rarely achieved, primarily because in order for cooperative learning to be successful, teachers must follow specific steps, carefully organizing the content and skills that students are to "teach" each other. (After all, the students do not know this material as well as the teacher does.) They must group students carefully with regard to academic ability, race, and gender; place students in groups of four or five students with a high, a low, and two or three medium-achieving students in each group; and compute student "improvement scores," an essential component in Slavin's work. In computing improvement scores, the teacher must first compute base scores for each student and for each group of students from past quizzes and tests. They then need to administer the test or quiz again to the class and convert the scores to improvement points.

Failing at any one step could jeopardize the results that had been achieved when the approach was studied. Yet, few teachers follow all these steps. While some choose occasional group work, most do not do anything resembling the cooperative learning described in the literature—mostly because these well-intentioned techniques have been tried and have failed in practice. Instead, most social studies teachers discover on their own that teacher-centered techniques are among the best ways to improve student learning. This happens despite the fact that cooperative learning and similar student-centered approaches are stressed repeatedly in initial teacher training programs and at numerous professional conferences and workshops. Teachers reject these approaches because they conduct a common sense, cost benefit analysis. The costs of student-centered approaches are high, immediate, and certain. The most obvious costs are additional time to prepare such lessons and additional class time. To many teachers, the benefits of student-centered approaches—eventually improving student achievement appear to be highly uncertain and distant. As a result, many place their faith in teacher-centered approaches.

Of course, either knowing that a classroom is student-centered or knowing that it is teacher-centered reveals little about the quality of instruction in the classroom. It tells nothing about the facts and concepts being presented, examples being used, or interaction between teacher and students. Teachers who favor teacher-centered approaches, however, tend to focus on what content to teach, the sequence of ideas, the examples used, the demonstrations performed, the questions asked, and the students' responses, and they tend to be more interested in the details of instruction—all central components of effective teaching.

In any case, regardless of one's personal preference for student- or teacher-centered instruction, the ultimate questions should be: What are the results of instruction? Do students achieve more? Under what conditions is learning enhanced? Research consistently shows that, while student-centered instruction may work in some cases, teacher-centered instruction works better with most students and with most teachers. Unfortunately, this is precisely what the leaders of the field who are focused on promoting student-centered methods ignore.

WHAT DO SOCIAL STUDIES TEACHING METHODS BOOKS TEACH?

Though there is evidence that many teachers, parents, and administrators prefer teacher-centered instruction, leaders of the field still work overtime to push student-centered learning. In fact, today's teaching methods textbooks in social studies are nearly silent on how to develop teacher-led, teacher-centered instruction. Instead, the authors of these books are deeply influenced by the progressive legacy of student-centered instruction.

Some early methods books do provide a more balanced approach. Lee Ehman, Howard Mehlinger and John Patrick's (1974) book *Toward Effective Instruction in Secondary Social Studies*, for example, has some positive things to say about teacher presentations. The index shows nine references to expository instruction. The book devotes 10 full pages to expository instruction, giving advice on how to plan and deliver a good lecture. Prospective teachers are advised to begin a lesson by explaining what students are expected to learn. Then they define unfamiliar ideas or facts, proceed in a well-organized manner, provide immediate corrections to students, and close by reviewing the ideas that were taught.

Most methods books from the latter half of the last century, however, give short shrift to teacher-centered methods. Edgar B. Wesley's 1950 book, *Teaching Social Studies in High Schools*, includes just seven references to lecture. And, though he discusses what lectures are and explains how many social studies teachers use "informal" lectures, the discussion is couched in his distaste for such teacher-centered methods: "the teacher who lectures in the public schools is likely to be charged with . . . cruelty to pupils." In another example, Maurice P. Hunt and Lawrence E. Metcalf's 1968 book, *Teaching High School Social Studies*, includes neither the phrase "direct instruction" nor the word "lecture" in the index.

The book is, however, filled with references to "reflective thought" and issues related to power, class, and race.

Additional evidence of the disproportionate emphasis on student-centered instruction can be found in the *Handbook of Research on Social Studies Teaching and Learning*. This is regarded as a highly authoritative, landmark work in the field. Edited by James P. Shaver (1931), it includes 53 chapters. These carefully selected and meticulously edited chapters address numerous concerns in social studies education. Yet, the index has a single reference to direct instruction—Peter Martorella mentions it in his chapter on teaching concepts, devoting four paragraphs (in a book of over 600 pages) to this form of teaching. Even here, though, there is no respect for teacher-centered instruction. Martorella summarizes the work of Barak Rosenshine but then dismisses it. He explains that teacher-centered instruction is only useful for low-level cognitive objectives and probably not worth employing in social studies classrooms.

Perhaps most disturbing is that these are not isolated instances of neglect. In fact, a brief review of the most widely used social studies methods textbooks exposes a widespread disregard for direct instruction.

• In Jack Zevin's (2000) *Social Studies for the Twenty-First Century: Methods and Materials for Teaching in Middle and Secondary Schools*, neither the phrase "direct instruction" nor the word "lecture" appears in the index. Didactic roles of teachers are described but such roles receive short shrift and little enthusiasm when compared to descriptions of "reflective" and "affective" roles. Didactic approaches are described in order to be contrasted with other, better approaches. Zevin never suggests how to plan and deliver any sort of teacher-led presentation.

• Peter H. Martorella's (2001) *Teaching Social Studies in Middle and Secondary Schools* follows a similar pattern. Neither the phrase "direct instruction" nor the word "lecture" appears in the index. Little attention is given to how such teacher-centered instruction might work or what research might support such an approach. Even a short section on expository approaches turns out to supply scant advice on what such instruction might entail.

• In Thomas L. Dynneson and Richard E. Gross's (1999) *Designing Effective Instruction for Secondary Social Studies*, neither the phrase "direct instruction" nor the word "lecture" appears in the index. Nearly every sort of instruction is described, including suggestions for using technology, motivating students, and teaching about values. A single paragraph is devoted to giving a lecture.

• In Walter C. Parker's (2001) *Social Studies in Elementary Education*, neither the phrase "direct instruction" nor the word "lecture" appears in the index. By contrast, cooperative learning, curriculum integration, and literacy have whole chapters of their own.

• George W. Maxim's (2003) *Dynamic Social Studies for Elementary Classrooms* is the exception. He includes a chapter called "direct instruction." While constructivism and other incongruencies are also included in this chapter, Maxim is clear about the important role of instruction wherein the teacher presents lessons to the whole class, provides immediate feedback, and monitors student performance. He is also clear that teachers need a deep understanding of factual information if they are to be successful direct instruction teachers.

These examples clearly illustrate that teaching methods textbooks in social studies are nearly silent on how to develop teacher led, teacher-centered instruction. The authors of these books are deeply influenced by the progressive legacy of student-centered instruction and they allow this influence to misrepresent social studies classrooms as student-centered, when in reality classroom observation suggests otherwise.

IS THE FAILURE TO PROMOTE TEACHER-CENTERED INSTRUCTION A PROBLEM?

Does the social studies establishment's attachment to student-centered approaches and the rejection of teacher-centered instruction cause problems? Yes, especially for beginning teachers. First-year teachers arrive each year in their classrooms ill prepared to teach. They know a few tricks. They know how to write an objective. If they are lucky, they know some of the state's social studies standards. They might understand Piaget's stages of cognitive development and Bloom's Taxonomy.

But it soon dawns on the fledging teachers that their students come to class every day, five days a week. High school teachers often see over 100 students each day. New teachers are often assigned the most difficult students. And deportment varies greatly. Some students won't stay in their seats. Others won't participate in groups—especially when the teacher assigns the group members. Some students become unruly. Fights break out. Other students sit quietly, using social studies time to finish their math assignments. Many won't work at all. Yet all look to the teacher for classroom leadership, subject knowledge, and classroom order—precisely the things for which most social studies teachers are not well trained. The methods they have been taught at the university—the vast majority of which are the student-centered approaches stressed in the college textbooks—are simply not equal to the task of real world teaching.

Where should first-year teachers turn for help? The culture of many high schools is like the TV show "Survivor." Experienced teachers, the very teachers who could help out the beginners, often resent sharing their experiences. After all, they learned how to teach the hard way. They struggled at first. It took them several years to discover what works. Why shouldn't today's newcomers do the same? The rookies should be "first off the island."

What are first-year teachers to do when the approaches taught by their professors of education fail them? For those who want to survive, the answer is simple. The new teachers have to train themselves—often by relying on trial and error—to find methods that truly work. Many will discover the benefits of teacher centered instruction on their own. This perhaps is the best that we could hope for, despite the fact that they will do many students little good in the first years of teaching.

Unfortunately, when the student-centered methods these teachers were taught fail, if teachers are not prepared to use the more rigorous and reliable teacher-centered methods, many beginning teachers will discover that they can manage a classroom better with "noninstruction." To be sure, these teachers will monitor students, assign seatwork and homework, but ultimately they will not impart much substantive knowledge and they will not challenge students to learn the content found in the readings, worksheets, and homework they assign. These teachers essentially give up on either teacher *or* student-centered instruction and merely "keep school." Noninstruction, after all, often leads to an orderly and tranquil classroom. It is a low-challenge environment to which many students and administrators would not object. If this happens, noninstruction may go unchallenged for years. Few incentives exist for principals to weed out poor teachers who actually manage their classrooms relatively well. Either way—whether beginning teachers discover teacher-centered instruction or noninstruction—the training these teachers received at colleges and universities failed them. They are left to train themselves.

The Cover-Up: Remedial Teacher Education

Up until now, we have somehow managed to avoid the worst consequences of failing to train teachers to use direct instruction. We have done so in part by expensive, stopgap measures: reducing class size to allow ill-trained teachers to more easily organize their classrooms so that more learning can eventually take place; assigning peer mentors to new teachers to pick up the slack for the education schools and train them in more effective teacher-centered instruction techniques. (Many large urban school districts have launched large-scale peer mentoring programs as a way to compensate for failures in teacher education.)

How long can the cover-up continue? Not forever. Most states are facing huge budget deficits and their ability to fully fund such policies as reduced class size and peer-mentoring programs may be severely limited. Moreover, by focusing on results rather than theories, the new accountability requirements of the No Child Left Behind Act make it difficult for colleges and universities as well as the public schools to cling to the failed approaches of the past. The widespread failure of teacher education is being exposed.

Results Should Matter

By holding schools and districts accountable for results, the federal No Child Left Behind Act shifts the education debate from an argument over which theory is better to an argument over what works. Unfortunately, this law currently only holds schools accountable for results in reading, math, and eventually science. Education leaders should extend these principles to social studies and should consider:

• Specifying academic levels of success for individual schools. Levels should include reference to student performance on state content tests and should take into account the value-added approaches used in some states. So, for example, high schools where 80 percent of the students are proficient or advanced in social studies at grade 8 might be classified as successful.

• Defining schools that have failed social studies programs in terms of specific student test results. So, for example, high schools where less than 80 percent of the students are proficient or advanced might be classified as failing.

• Offering financial incentives to assist failing schools that are willing to make changes. Principals and teachers in failing schools should be invited to study the programs at successful schools to see what these schools are doing right. They should imitate the schools that have been successful rather than set out in some new, experimental direction. If these formerly failing schools become successful, then they too should be eligible for additional funding to expand their programs. The cost of failure should be high. If schools fail after some specified period of time (e.g., two years?), they should be closed, reconstituted, or turned over to a charter school operator.

CONCLUSION

Teacher-centered instruction is supported by a strong set of empirical results conducted over several decades. And yet, these approaches are ignored by the leaders of the profession, as evidenced by the content in textbooks used to train teachers and in authoritative reviews of research. To discuss teacher-centered instruction is not even considered polite conversation. Nevertheless, now is the time for social studies leaders as well as legislators and parents to acknowledge the obvious weaknesses of student-centered approaches and begin to correct the excesses. We should acknowledge that poor teaching and learning do indeed exist in this field and, just as important, that it is not because of teacher-led, content-focused instruction. Results from the National Assessment of Educational Progress have shown repeatedly that U.S. students have scant understanding of history, geography, and civics. It is likely that this dismal state of affairs is the result of a century of ignoring content and promoting instructional practices with little chance of classroom success. The failure to improve academic achievement should be placed at the doorstep of the progressive theorists who brought us here and, just as important, are almost certainly incapable of leading us in a new direction. Perhaps an emphasis on results-oriented reforms can create a new energy in social studies to help us focus our attention on academic achievement rather than prolonging the endless debate between the advocates of teacher-centered and student-centered approaches in social studies.

References

Adams, G. and Engelmann, S. (1996). *Research on direct instruction: 20 years beyond DISTAR*. Seattle, WA: Educational Achievement Systems.

Cuban, L. (1991). History of Teaching in Social Studies. In Shaver, James P. (Ed.). *Handbook of research on social studies teaching and learning* (pp. 197-209). New York: MacMillan Publishing Company.

Dynneson, T.L. and Gross, R.E. (1999). *Designing effective instruction for secondary social studies*. Upper Saddle River, NJ: Merrill Prentice Hall.

Ehman, L., Mehlinger, H., and Patrick, J. (1974). *Toward effective instruction in secondary social studies*. Boston: Houghton Mifflin Company.

Goodlad, J.I. (1984). *A place called school*. New York: McGraw Hill Book Company.

Hirsch, E.D., Jr. (1996). *The schools we need and why we don't have them*. New York: Doubleday.

Hunt, M.P. and Metcalf, L.E. (1968). *Teaching high school social studies: Problems in reflective thinking and social understanding*. New York: Harper and Row.

Martorella, P.H. (1991). Knowledge and concept development in social studies. In Shaver, James P. (Ed.). *Handbook of research on social studies teaching and learning* (pp. 370-384). New York: MacMillan Publishing Company.

Martorella, P.H. (2001). *Teaching social studies in middle and secondary schools:* Upper Saddle River, NJ: Merrill Prentice Hall.

Maxim, G.W. (2003). *Dynamic social studies for elementary classrooms* (7th ed.). Upper Saddle River, NJ: Merrill Prentice Hall.

Parker, W.C. (2001). *Social studies in elementary education* (11th ed). Upper Saddle River, New Jersey: Merrill Prentice Hall.

Rosenshine, B. and Stevens, R. (1986). Teaching functions. In

Wittrock, M. C. (Ed.). *Handbook of Research on Teaching* (pp. 376-391). New York: MacMillan Publishing Company.

Schug, M.C. Tarver, S., and Western, R.D. (2001). *Direct instruction and the teaching of early reading: Wisconsin's teacher led insurgency.* Mequon, WI: Wisconsin Policy Research Institute.

Shaver, J.P. (1931). *The handbook of research on social studies teaching and learning.* New York: McMillan Publishing Company.

Slavin, R. (1990). *Cooperative learning: Theory, research and practice.* Englewood Cliffs, NJ: Prentice Hall.

Wesley, E.B. (1950). *Teaching social studies in high schools.* Boston: D.C. Heath.

Zevin, J. (2000). *Social studies for the twenty-first century: Methods and materials for teaching.* Mahwah: NJ: Lawrence Erlbaum Associates, Inc.

6

Garbage In, Garbage Out
Expanding environments, constructivism, and content knowledge in social studies

Bruce Frazee and Samuel Ayers

Imagine, for a moment, a child learning to play chess. Even if the child were old enough, and intellectually developed enough, to learn how to play chess, it would do no good to plunk him or her in front of a board and say, "Play the game." There is prior knowledge required; the rules of movement, orientation of the board, the function of each piece—each of these are pieces of knowledge you have to know to successfully play the game.

Once you know these things, you can begin to accrue strategies and tactics that will make you a master chess player by playing against other players. But if you don't know how to move your pieces, you're not apt to build your knowledge of chess. In chess, substantive content knowledge is the prerequisite for learning.

The same is true in education, and specifically in the social studies: you have to possess some basic skills and knowledge before you can begin to tackle the higher tasks of analysis and critical thinking. Content knowledge is also the backbone of good teaching. To be effective, pedagogy must begin by identifying the specific knowledge a teacher expects students to learn and establishing clear assessment procedures. Only then can teachers begin to determine *how* to teach content to their students.

Unfortunately, the delivery of content in elementary social studies is frequently hampered by two popular but misguided theories—"expanding environments" and "constructivism." Both are ineffective because they focus on how social studies should be taught in elementary classrooms rather than on the content knowledge that should be the centerpiece for teaching and learning.

Expanding environments is the basic curriculum that most states, textbook companies, and curriculum leaders use to organize elementary (K-6) social studies, and it has dominated elementary school social studies for nearly 75 years. The basic premise is that at each grade level, each year, students are exposed to a slowly widening social environment that takes up, in turn, self/home (kindergarten), families (1st grade), neighborhoods (2nd), communities (3rd), state (4th), country (5th), and world (6th). While this approach appears to provide an organized curricular sequence, it lacks substantial content, especially in the early elementary grades, and children tend to find its narrow focus deeply boring. In fact, expanding environments actually *impedes* content knowledge because of its trivial and repetitious sequence. For example, students in grades K-3 are taught about "community helpers" like mail carriers, milkmen, and fire fighters. Such lessons are superfluous (what kindergartener does not know about firefighters?) but more damagingly do not even begin to lay the groundwork for later study of history, heroes, struggles, victories, and defeats. Instead, they limit children's instruction to persons and institutions with which children are already familiar.

Constructivism is a theory that holds that humans learn when they analyze, interpret, create, and construct meaning from experience and knowledge. At its root is a belief that only self-discovered knowledge is understood and remembered. Constructivists believe that students must be self-directed while learning in order to create their own meaningful experiences that will be retained when moving forward in life. While there is no doubt that some worthwhile learning may occur this way, it is difficult, if not impossible, to achieve self-created meaning unless specific content knowledge is a prerequisite.

Proponents of both approaches—expanding environments and constructivism—stress the importance of active learning over content knowledge as a necessary component of historical or geographical understanding. Yet just as the chess player needs to know how to move the pieces before he or she can begin the process of mastering chess, the elementary student needs content knowledge as the basis of thinking critically about history, civics, geography, economics, and all the other disciplines that make up the social studies. Content knowledge, we argue, must come first when making teaching and learning decisions.

EXPANDING ENVIRONMENTS IN ELEMENTARY SCHOOL SOCIAL STUDIES

The scope and sequence of elementary social studies in American schools has seen little substantive change in three quarters of a century. As Maxim (1991) comments, "No one knows exactly how this system first evolved, but some time during the 1930s an organizational pattern emerged" (p. 21). Although several individuals and events contributed to its formation, this durable curriculum is most closely associated with educator Paul Hanna. The sequence is known by a jumble of vague names, including "expanding environments," "expanding horizons," "expanding communities," "widening horizons," "expanding interests," "widening interests," and—Paul Hanna's favorite term—"expanding communities of men." LeRiche (1987) summarizes the concept in this way: "The basic idea is that the child's understanding grows like a set of widening concentric circles and that the child should study social life based on this presumed sequence of conceptual development" (p. 139). Following this theory, elementary students are to begin their formal social studies experiences by studying themselves and other people influencing their lives, then gradually enlarge the circle.

William Kilpatrick, Harold Rugg, and John Dewey, all influential progressive educators of the 1920s and 1930s, helped lead the charge to revise the K-12 curriculum by replacing the study of history and heroes with a new focus on social, political, and economic problems. Ravitch (1987) explains that they sought "to make the curriculum less academic, more utilitarian, less 'subject-centered,' and more closely related to students' interests and experiences" (p. 345).

As a graduate student and young college faculty member, Hanna was greatly influenced by Kilpatrick, Rugg, and Jesse Newlon, a trio that Stallones (1999) says exposed Hanna to social reconstructionism. Hanna then served as a consultant on the social studies for Virginia, where he was instrumental in social studies curriculum reform in that state. According to Gill (1974), the new curriculum replaced history, civics, and geography with a study of "unitary life experiences" emphasizing human relationships. First grade students studied relationships within the home and school, second grade students studied relationships in the neighborhood, third grade students studied environmental forces in the community, and fourth grade students studied exploration and settlement. The sequence was eventually dubbed "expanding horizons" or "expanding environments."

As one of the primary advocates of this new elementary social studies curriculum, Hanna became identified with the broader social studies movement, which emphasized everyday life and problem solving. Gill (1974) states that Hanna's professional association with Scott Foresman and Company led to his development of a formal K-12 social studies program consisting of textbooks and student activity suggestions for early elementary grades, which proved to be a financial success. Over the course of his career, Hanna continually promoted expanding environments and exerted national influence on both colleges of education and textbook publishers.

Today expanding environments continues to dominate elementary social studies programs, textbooks, and social studies methods courses that thousands of future teachers take each year. Welton (2002) notes, "You may find occasional variations on the expanding-environments approach to social studies, but for all practical purposes it is a national curriculum" (p. 70). Ravitch (1987) points out, "So widespread is this pattern in American public schools that one might assume that this particular sequence represents the accumulated wisdom of generations of educational research" (p. 345), even though it is based on a philosophy of learning rather than research in cognitive psychology or child development.

CRITICISM OF EXPANDING ENVIRONMENTS

For the past several decades, many educators have criticized expanding environments for its lack of substantive content knowledge. The first three years, for example, are simply repetition, since the family, neighborhood, and community are topics children know before coming to school. Larkins et al. (1987) assert that much of the K-3 social studies curriculum is "redundant, superfluous, and needlessly superficial" and blame "adherence to the sequence of family, neighborhood, community . . . for the trivialization of social studies in the first three grades" (p. 300). By limiting the curriculum to persons and institutions directly relevant to the student, expanding environments precludes many high interest historical figures, significant events, meaningful achievements, and diverse cultures. Veteran teachers Gwen Souter and Shelly Reid (personal communication, November 25, 2002) state that "the traditional social studies curriculum focusing on self, neighborhood, and community helpers is just plain boring. The typical daycare, preschool, and Sunday school curricula all have a similar focus on self. Such a curriculum is repetitive and of low interest to young school children." Zarrillo (2000) contends, "Devoting four grades to family, school, and community provides children with too limited a view" (p. 17). The dull nature of expanding horizons influences many elementary teachers to simply spend little or no classroom time on any social studies topics.

More importantly, as Rooze and Foerster (1972) note, the expanding environments sequence is based on a faulty assumption: that children can only understand the environment nearest in time and space to their personal experiences. This assumption ignores the vast exposure to media that is a hallmark of modern childhood, which greatly increases a child's experiential base. J.S. Leming (personal communication, November 23, 2002) points out that this organizational approach, if applied to science education, would dictate that children should learn about cockroaches rather than dinosaurs since bugs are closer to their experience base and they are limited in their ability to comprehend subjects so far removed in time and space—a nonsensical notion, as anyone who has taken children to a natural history museum can attest.

In fact, expanding environments not only impedes the acquisition of knowledge, it is actually based on a rather questionable reading of child developmental psychology. Joseph Adelson (quoted in Bennett, 1988), professor of psychology at the University of Michigan, contends, "There is nothing in the cognitive science, or in developmental research, which supports the present way of doing things" (p. 26). Akenson (1987) points out that while young students may need to begin with the simple and move to the complex, "dependency upon developmental psychology, interpretations of what constitute children's immediate experiences and interests, the artificially happy and conflict free picture of society, and the manner in which the social world presents itself to children suggest flaws of major dimensions" (p. 169).

Despite these criticisms, the National Council for the Social Studies (NCSS) continues to support expanding environments as the preferred scope and sequence for elementary social studies programs. The NCSS Task Force on Scope and Sequence affirmed this approach in 1983 and again in 1989 and continued its advocacy of expanding horizons. While three alternative curriculum models for social studies were also endorsed, none offered a radical departure from the traditional framework. Maxim (1991) explains that, "Reaction to the report of the Task Force on Scope and Sequence was divided. . . . Despite its vocal dissenters, the expanding environments approach remains the overwhelming choice for curriculum organization among social studies program developers and textbook publishers today" (p. 23).

Why does expanding environments endure among textbook companies, in college social studies methods classes, and in the elementary curriculum? Akenson (1989) attributes the persistent dominance of expanding environments to "cultural, bureaucratic, and economic realities" (p. 50) that make entrenched groups prefer the status quo. Textbook publishers have made a profit addressing these topics for decades; teacher educators have been comfortable endorsing this sequence in social studies methods textbooks and in their classrooms; and teachers and parents have simply accepted the supposed expertise of this textbook-driven sequence.

CONSTRUCTIVISM

Constructivism is a method of instruction based on a descriptive theory about the thought processes involved in learning. It is deeply popular among educators—so popular, in fact, that few have stopped to consider that in this case, the emperor has no clothes.

Few practitioners know or understand the varied and confusing applications and interpretations of constructivism. Bredo (2000) notes that constructivism is a massive logical feedback loop; any attempt to define constructivism "that does not take into account the variety in definitions will itself be a created construct; constructivism is its own first problem" (p. 128). Airasian and Walsh (1997) comment that "constructivism is not an instructional approach; it is a theory about how learners come to know. Although instructional approaches are typically derived from such epistemologies, they are distinct from them" (pp. 444-445).

No matter that few know (or care) what constructivism is. It remains popular with many professors and authors of social studies methods textbooks because it is somehow thought to account for the process of student learning. Again, left aside in the perplexing descriptions and definitions of constructivism is the importance and necessity of content knowledge. Constructivism also complicates the teacher's role in teaching and implementing elementary school social studies. A review of the definitions and descriptions of constructivism points to the problem.

TYPES OF CONSTRUCTIVISM

Amid the cacophony, two types of constructivism stand out. The first is cognitive constructivism, based on Piaget's theory of developmental stages. He believed that cognitive development facilitates learning through actively involving the learner, and that learning can only occur when the child is at the appropriate cognitive development stage. Cognitive constructivists believe that students move through developmental stages that enable them to experience reality through active learning. The teacher's role is to facilitate student learning by challenging a student's reality through active experiences and the creation of new ideas (Piaget, p. 122).

The second, even more opaque, type of constructivism is based on Vygotsky's belief that social interaction is crucial for learning. Vygotsky (p. 122) identifies two mechanisms for acquiring knowledge: "scaffolding" and "zone of proximal development." Scaffolding provides temporary support for the child until the child is capable of doing a given task alone. The zone of proximal development provides learning through social interaction experiences. Social constructivists believe that if a child is within the zone of proximal development and has scaffolding, he or she can learn anything. They believe that teachers must collaborate with students during learning, since social interaction is the key ingredient to learning. These two types of constructivist theories require elementary social studies teachers to adapt to a variety of new active and social roles emphasizing process over content.

CONSTRUCTIVISM IN SOCIAL STUDIES TEACHING

Education journals add to the confusion surrounding constructivism. Writers use a welter of jargon to describe the many roles of a constructivist teacher in a social studies classroom. All serve to emphasize the social aspect of teaching and learning with little recognition of the importance of content knowledge in the teaching process. For example, Scheurman (1998) offers a hierarchy of jargon to label and describe constructivist teachers. One type of teacher is a *transmitter* (behaviorist) who presents information in small parts to students through listening, lecturing, rehearsing, and reciting. Transmitter teachers are criticized for stressing right and wrong answers and not promoting student involvement. Far more preferable are *managers* (information processors), who assist students in gathering and processing information. The teacher as manager helps students connect to prior knowledge by "chunking" information so students can use their own thought processes. Scheurman also describes the teacher as *facilitator* (cognitive constructivism) or *collaborator* (social constructivism). The facilitator challenges and guides students while monitoring their reflective thinking. The collaborator participates with students in constructing their reality using open-ended strategies and authentic resources. Scheurman concedes that factual knowledge plays a role in learning. "For example," he writes, "it is difficult to imagine any learning encounter without a certain transmission of knowledge on the part of the teacher—even the most collaborative exercise requires instructions and prerequisite information" (p. 8). Constructivist education professors tend to overlook the last part of this quotation in their enthusiasm for collaborative and facilitative learning methods.

In another article intended for educators, Scheurman and Newmann (1998) describe three criteria to guide teachers in evaluating their own and their students' work. They state, "[R]ather than assume that either response—transmission teaching or doing constructivism—will achieve the goals of social education, we believe it is necessary to first articulate criteria for authentic intellectual achievement, and then to see what practices tend to result in student performances that meet those criteria" (p. 23). Newmann, Marks, and Gamoran (1996) describe the teacher's role as a "cognitive apprenticeship" in a social setting. Here the teacher guides the student to make choices for discovering information.

Put aside the fact that this flurry of jargon wraps the profession of teaching in a fog so thick as to be impenetrable. These constructivist descriptions of teacher roles constitute unrealistic expectations for both teachers and students. Teachers become so engaged in the active social constructivist role that the content knowledge crucial to the success of these "experiences" is lost. In short, everyone is so caught up in structuring a learning environment no one gives much thought to what is—or is not—*actually learned*.

The damage to children is far worse, however. Elementary students have limited experiences and knowledge and few are mature enough to determine what they need to learn. Yet constructivism plays a dirty little trick on them by shifting responsibility for creating and acquiring knowledge from the teacher to the learner regardless of age, background, or experience. Does the child know little or nothing about history, civics, or geography? Well, the child must be developmentally late, or perhaps incapable of "self-direction." Off to special ed with him. Since the teacher is merely a "cognitive coach" and is not responsible for selecting and transmitting appropriate knowledge, you can't pin on the teacher a student's failure to construct meaning.

Teacher preparation programs promote constructivism by disguising it as teaching "best practices," or by describing it with such popular slogans as "discovery learning" and "self-directed learning." Of course, a variety of methods are necessary to deliver content knowledge that engages students successfully in learning. We are not opposed to imaginative ways of reinforcing learning. But again, the key ingredient for constructed meaning is content knowledge. Without such knowledge, it is impossible for students to engage in the higher order thinking and critical analysis that purveyors of constructivism claim as the goal of this method.

For example, teachers who have students make pyramids from sugar cubes, create Native American necklaces from macaroni, or build Conestoga wagons from Popsicle sticks (all methods solidly within the constructivist model) without actually teaching students about Egypt, Native American cultures, or the frontier inhibit understanding and create inaccurate associations. Not to sound pedantic, but the Egyptians did not build pyramids from sugar cubes. Students need to know first about Egyptian culture to make such a project relevant—if it is at all.

Constructivism will increasingly find itself at odds with the standards and testing movement as the latter gathers momentum among policy makers and parents. Constructivism has no value to the standards movement without the acknowledgment of the importance of building and increasing a substantive and meaningful content knowledge base.

No one can deny that children simply don't know enough about history, civics, and geography. The National Assessment of Educational Progress results, along with lesser-known studies, have indicated for years that most American children leave elementary school with little knowledge of these critical subjects. As long as social studies leaders tolerate the expanding environments curriculum and promote social constructivism without emphasizing content knowledge, the situation is unlikely to improve. A radical overhaul of the social studies is needed—one that gives children the tools they need, in the form of actual content knowledge, and jettisons faulty approaches built on questionable theories like expanding environments and constructivism.

REFERENCES

Airasian, P.W., and Walsh, M.E. (1997). Constructivist cautions. *Phi Delta Kappan,* 78(9), 444-449.

Akenson, J. E. (1989). The expanding environments and elementary education: A critical perspective. *Theory and Research in Social Education,* 17(1), 33-52.

Akenson. J.E. (1987). Historical factors in the development of elementary social studies: Focus on the expanding environments. *Theory and Research in Social Education,* 15(3), 55-171.

Bennett, W. (1986). First lessons. *Phi Delta Kappan,* 68, 125-129.

Bennett, W. (1988). *James Madison Elementary School: A curriculum for American students.* Washington, DC: U.S. Department of Education.

Bredo, E. (2000). Reconsidering social constructivism: The relevance of George Herbert Mead's interactionism. In D.C. Phillips (Ed.). *Constructivism in education* (pp. 127-158). Chicago, IL: University of Chicago Press.

Brooks, J.G., and Brooks, M.G. (1993). *In search of understanding: The case for constructivist classrooms.* Alexandria, VA: Association for Supervision and Curriculum Development.

Hanna, P.R. (1963). Revising the social studies: What is needed? *Social Education,* 27 190-196.

Hanna, P.R. (1965). Design for a social studies program. In *Focus on the social studies: A report from Department of Elementary School Principals* (pp. 228-245). Washington, DC: National Educational Association.

Larkins, A.G., Hawkins, M.L., and Gilmore, A. (1987). Trivial and noninformative content of elementary social studies: A review of primary texts in four states. *Theory and Research in Social Education,* 15(4), 299-311.

LeRiche, L.W. (1987). The expanding environments sequence in elementary social studies: The origins. *Theory and Research in*

Social Studies, 15(3), 37-154.

Gill, M. (1974). *Paul R. Hanna: The evolution of an elementary social studies textbook series.* Unpublished doctoral dissertation, Northwestern University.

Maxim, G.W. (1991). *Social studies and the elementary school child, Sixth Edition.* Upper Saddle River, NJ: Merrill.

Newmann, F.M., Marks, H.M., and Gamoran, A. (1996). Authentic pedagogy and student performance. *American Journal of Education,* 104, 1-312.

Piaget, J. (1929). *The child's conception of the world.* New York: Harcourt Brace and Co.

Piaget, J. (1970). *The science of education and the psychology of the child.* New York: Grossman.

Ravitch, D. (1987). Tot sociology: Or what happened to history in the grade schools. *American Scholar,* 56(3), 343-355.

Rooze, G.E., and Foerster, L.M. (1972). *Teaching elementary social studies: A new perspective.* Columbus, OH: Charles E. Merrill Publishing Company.

Scheurman, G. (1998). From behaviorist to constructivist teaching. *Social Education,* 62(1), 6-9.

Scheurman, G. and Newmann, F. M. (1998). Authentic intellectual work in social studies: Putting performance before pedagogy. *Social Education,* 62(1), 23-35.

Stallones, J.R. (1999). *The life and work of Paul Robert Hanna.* Unpublished doctoral dissertation, University of Texas, Austin TX.

Stanley, G.K. (2001). Faith without works: twenty-five years of undervaluing content area knowledge. *Educational Horizons,* 80, 24-27.

Vygotsky, L.S. (1978). *Mind in society.* Cambridge, MA: Harvard University Press.

Welton, D.A. (2002). *Children and their world: Strategies for teaching social studies*, Seventh Edition. Boston, MA: Houghton Mifflin.

Zarrillo, (2000). *Teaching elementary social studies: principles and applications.* Upper Saddle River, NJ: Merrill Publishing Company.

7

Ignorant Activists

Social change, "higher order thinking," and the failure of social studies[1]

James S. Leming

A core belief among contemporary social studies educators is that in order to promote the capacity for citizenship one must educate youth to think critically about public policy issues. It is argued that citizens of a democracy must decide what positions to hold on major public policy issues of the day. From the inception of social studies in the early years of the 20th century, this impulse to infuse the subject with controversial public issues has shaped the field's development. In this chapter, I examine this idea and show how it has served to weaken both the practice of effective social studies education and the preparation of future citizens. In brief, my argument is that this use of social studies as a vehicle for promoting social change has rested on faulty assumptions about the intellectual capacities of youth and has deflected social studies leaders' attention away from the important role of developing students' understandings of important subject matter in history, geography, economics, and civics. I conclude that this impulse has contributed to a curricular field that is in a state of crisis, lacking both solid curricula and effective pedagogy. I turn first to the roots and underlying ideology of this perspective and its development.

HISTORICAL PERSPECTIVE

An important milestone in the history of the school curriculum was the *Report of the Committee on Social Studies* (Dunn, 1916). It urged a new synthesis of subjects that included history (ancient to current U.S.), civics, geography, and economics. The proposed integration was designed to refocus the study of such subjects on current issues, social problems, and the needs and interests of students and their communities. In the end, this would gravely change the traditional disciplines.

In the 1920s, the national debate about the purpose of education focused upon whether it should emphasize socialization and the transmission of traditions, or developing in students the desire and skills to help create a new social order. It is a tribute to the persuasiveness of its arguments that the 1916 committee report effectively won the hearts and minds of at least one segment of the population: the intellectual leaders of the educational profession. A typical example of that era's readiness to jettison tradition can be found in a statement by the Superintendent of the Denver Public Schools in the *Tenth Yearbook of the Department of Superintendence of the National Education Association* (Threlkeld, 1931):

> The whole of this tradition (relying upon great thinkers and traditions) is warped by the vicious assumption that each generation will live substantially amid the conditions governing the lives of its fathers and will transmit those conditions to mold with equal force the lives of its children. *We are living in the first period of human history for which this assumption is false.* Relativity must replace absolutism in the realm of morals as well as in the spheres of physics and biology (p. 23, italics added).

It was also the judgment of many educational theorists in the 1920s and 1930s that the American experiment in democracy and free markets was faltering. To educate children by teaching only respect for the nation's cultural heritage would not advance the new social order that was urgently needed. How then was the curriculum to be organized, especially that part of it where the cultural heritage was most embedded? By reconceptualizing the social studies curriculum as interdisciplinary and focusing its goals on social change, education theorists of the era hoped they could break the grip of cultural tradition with its emphasis on rugged individualism and ensure that the curriculum would instead serve to advance a more collective social order.

The full flowering of this "progressive" view of the social studies curriculum occurred in the 1930s with the success of Harold Rugg's junior high school textbook series, *Man and His Changing Society*. It sold 1,317,960 books and 2,867,000 workbooks between 1929 and 1939 (Winters, 1967). Rugg's goal was to rid social studies of disciplinary compartments. From his perspective, the curriculum should instead focus pupil attention on contemporary problems, teach students to become aware and critical of social and economic injustices, and encourage them to participate actively in bringing about needed changes. Themes in the Rugg textbook series included the excesses of laissez faire capitalism, unfair distribution of income and wealth, unemployment, class conflict, immigration, rapid cultural change, and imperialism. Their presentation included thought provoking questions designed to encourage students to criticize selected aspects of contemporary society and tradition. Rugg and other progressives of that era hoped that students would thereby become aware of society's many flaws and develop a desire to ameliorate those ills, thus making it difficult, if not impossible, for the curriculum to instill a spirit of nationalism or respect for American culture.

Even while progressive educational practice experienced a temporary decline in the 1950s, this vision for social studies was kept alive in Hunt and Metcalf's (1955, 1968) *Teaching High School Social Studies* methods textbook. They argued that the problem areas in contemporary American culture (referred to as "closed areas") were saturated with prejudice and taboos. In order to become a more democratic society, they argued, it was necessary for social studies teachers to expose these areas to rational inquiry in their classrooms. The closed areas included in their textbook were power and the law, economic inequities, nationalism and patriotism, social class, religion and morality, race, and sexual morality. One finds little difference in the basic approach of Rugg and Hunt and Metcalf except that Rugg's focus was on the school curriculum while Hunt and Metcalf focused on training social studies teachers.

The progressive impulse in social studies education has survived and remains a strong characteristic of the field today. In 2003, the official National Council for the Social Studies definitional statement contains a strong interdisciplinary focus as well as a continuing preoccupation with solving social ills and downplaying subject matter:

> ... the integrated study of the social sciences and humanities to promote civic competence." Within the school program, social studies provides coordinated, systematic study drawing upon such disciplines as anthropology, archaeology, economics, geography, history, law, philosophy, political science, psychology, religion, and sociology, as well as appropriate content from the humanities, mathematics, and natural sciences. In essence, social studies promotes knowledge of and involvement in civic affairs. And because civic issues—such as health care, crime, and foreign policy—are multidisciplinary in nature, understanding these issues and *developing resolutions to them* (italics added) require multidisciplinary education. These characteristics are the key defining aspects of social studies.

Thus, 87 years after the appearance of the 1916 report, the nation's leading professional social studies organization defines the field in a way that subordinates content knowledge to a focus on solving society's ills. It is to both the practicality of such a focus and its deleterious consequences for history and social science instruction that I now turn.

CONTROVERSIAL PUBLIC ISSUES

Despite the repeated calls for social studies to teach students to think critically about social issues, achieving this objective has been elusive. In what follows, I try to explain why efforts to teach thinking in secondary social studies classrooms have been unsuccessful. I then outline what social studies can reasonably achieve in the development of thoughtfulness in students.

The "public issues" approach is arguably the most influential attempt to teach thinking in social studies. It emerged from the Harvard Social Studies Project (Oliver and Shaver, 1966). Rather than using a general model of reasoning, its proponents advocated engaging youth in open and critical discourse about public affairs and required students to draw upon historical and social science knowledge to reach defensible positions on issues of public concern. To demonstrate higher order thinking on a public policy task, students are expected to clearly state the issue, move beyond initial "nonreflective" positions, examine the facts of a case, elaborate the reasons behind a point of view, critically challenge the thinking and assumptions of others, and draw systematically on ethical and legal principles to develop a defensible position of their own. The important question is whether it is possible, through educational interventions, to produce in school-aged youth the advanced forms of thoughtfulness required by public policy analysis. I now turn to the evidence on this question.

THREE CONTROLLED STUDIES

A brief review of three efforts to teach students the skills associated with the analysis of controversial public issues illustrates both the curricular approach and the difficulties associated with attempting to effect changes in adolescents' ways of thinking via educational interventions.

As part of an evaluation of the Harvard Social Studies Project, four project members taught junior high school classes for extended periods of time throughout two school years. In these classes, a political analysis model was taught where students explored how different positions on public issues might be justified within a framework of constitutional principles. In this study, approximately half of the instructional time in social studies classes was devoted to public issues instruction. When program effects were evaluated, students in experimental classes were able to describe and identify the components of quality arguments when compared to control classes. However, on the most revealing form of assessment—student ability to state and support a decision on a public issue in student-led discussions—experimental pupils failed to improve upon prior performance. The research team conjectured that perhaps people ". . . develop persuasive arguments not because of the soundness of logic, but because of more general temperamental factors such as verbal fluency or interpersonal competence" (Oliver and Shaver, 1966, p. 324).

Another study, the *Higher Order Thinking in the Humanities Project* (Newmann, 1991), investigated department-wide efforts to teach higher order thinking in social studies classrooms. Newmann found that considerable difficulties exist even in attempting to locate such classrooms and assessing the impact of such curricula. Following a national search, nine social studies departments were identified that were judged to have made department-wide efforts to promote higher order thinking; seven other departments that made no such efforts were used for comparison purposes.

To determine whether higher order thinking was being taught in the identified classrooms, students were asked to write a persuasive essay using such skills and addressing whether a student's rights were violated in the case of a locker search that turned up a small amount of marijuana. Newmann (1991b) was not able to identify any substantial relationship between the presence of classroom thoughtfulness and pupil performance on the locker search essay. Generic qualities of classroom thoughtfulness were not found to be associated with persuasiveness of student writing on a constitutional issue. Given the great care that this study utilized to identify "thoughtful" classrooms, this finding must be accorded great weight.

The evaluation of the "You Decide" segments in Channel One television programming also produced no evidence that educators know how to systematically teach critical thinking about public policy issues (Johnston, Anderman, Klenk, and Harris, 1994). In the 1992-1993 broadcast season, Channel One created 14 "You Decide" segments covering selected news events that had clear public issues foci. Eight experienced teachers were trained in the "discussion of public issues" approach and, for a three-month period, they led at least two classroom discussions per week based on taped "You Decide" segments. The goal of this intervention was to teach students how to discuss controversial issues using oral strategies designed to facilitate thorough explorations of public policy issues.

To assess students' competency in the use of these public issues discussion skills, students (experimental and control) in groups of five to seven participated in videotaped sessions on the topic of prayer in schools. No statistically significant difference was detected between experimental students and control students on their use of public policy issues discussion skills. Researchers discovered that students simply presented their own unsubstantiated position, made passing reference to arguments presented by experts or the facts of the case, and did not work toward a defensible group position on the issue.

Something disturbing is implied by the findings of these three studies. If the development of student decision making abilities to be applied to the analysis of public policy issues is at the heart of social studies, and there is no evidence that these objectives are being achieved, what are the implications? Should social studies teachers drop the current project of teaching for thoughtful citizenship, reanalyze their expectations, and downscale their goals? Or, should they redouble their efforts to teach higher order thinking? I find problematic the very notion that adolescents can systematically be taught higher order thinking about complex public policy issues that perplex their parents.

The most common explanation offered by social studies theorists for why schools haven't been successful in teaching higher order thinking focus on teacher, curricular, and institutional factors. This perspective is, to use a medical analogy, similar to affirming that "the patient failed to respond" rather than "I misdiagnosed" or "I misprescribed." The presumption is that barriers to the teaching of higher order thinking are embedded in the organizational context of schools, not in the assumptions upon which the instructional model is based. Onosko (1991) has argued that such factors as pressure on teachers to focus on student knowledge acquisition, low expectations of students, large classes, and lack of teacher planning time stand in the way of achieving this goal. Such obstacles, though perhaps valid to some extent, do not constitute a complete picture of the difficulties encountered in teaching higher order thinking. There is a basic flaw in the underlying assumption of Controversial Public Issues (CPI) pedagogy. It is found in the assumption that, if one only engages students in thinking, they will develop higher order thinking skills.

CPI PEDAGOGY AND ADOLESCENT DEVELOPMENT

A critical weakness of CPI instruction is its fallacious assumption that school-aged students are capable of the cognitive tasks required by curricula intended to develop higher order thinking. This may help explain teachers' low expectations about students' critical thinking. Research findings on epistemological development indicate a progression in people's assumptions about sources and certainty of knowledge and how decisions are justified in light of those assumptions (King and Kitchener, 1994; Kitchener and King, 1981, 1985). The reflective judgment model of King and Kitchener depicts the development of people's assumptions about knowledge and how they radically affect the way individuals understand and solve problems. People at various developmental stages have differing assumptions about the roles of evidence, authority, and interpretation in the formation of solutions to problems and about what can be known and how certain one can be about knowing.

Research spanning 20 years, using longitudinal data as well as cross sectional studies, offers strong support for the existence of stages of development that are identifiable, age-related, and change in predictable ways over time (King and Kitchener, 1994). Data on stages of reflective judgment are collected through the Reflective Judgment Interview (RJI). The RJI presents respondents with four problems where some of the elements of a solution are unknown or not known with a specifiable degree of certainty. One such problem is the Chemical Additives Problem:

> There have been frequent reports about the relationship between chemicals that are added to foods and the safety of these foods. Some studies indicate that such chemicals can cause cancer, making these foods unsafe to eat. Other studies, however, show that chemical additives are not harmful, and actually make the foods containing them safer to eat.

Using a semi-structured interview format, respondents are asked a series of questions that require them to respond using their existing repertoire of cognitive skills. Typical probe questions ask respondents to present their resolution to the problem, relate how they came to that point of view, assess whether they can know for sure that their position is correct, relate their opinion on how differences of opinion would be adjudicated, and discuss how different people, especially experts, might come to hold differing opinions. Transcribed interviews are scored according to protocols (Kitchener and King, 1985).

Changes in reasoning are described by seven distinct sets of assumptions about knowledge and its acquisition. School-aged youth typically reason at either stage two or three. At stage two, there is a true reality that can be known with certainty but is not known by everyone. Beliefs are justified by direct observation and by what authorities say is true. At stage three, in areas where truth is known, one defers to known authorities. In areas where truth is not known, there is no basis for evaluation beyond one's intuitions or feelings. The solution to problems, therefore, is simply a matter of "opinion"—feelings—and one need not look beyond oneself for justification or warrant.

At stage four, for the first time, ill-structured problems are afforded legitimacy; that is, problems exist that cannot be described completely and solved with certainty. At this stage, truth is impossible to attain and therefore is idiosyncratic to the individual. Research on the development of reflective judgment suggests that high school seniors are typically at stage three in epistemic development. Prior to age 24, few individuals operate at stage four or higher (King and Kitchener, 1994).

If stage four reasoning is required for the solution of ill-structured problems, typical high school students will not accept the legitimacy of the task of searching for qualified positions on such tasks because most high school students simply cannot produce this form of reasoning. Research has shown that individuals are seldom able to produce reasoning that is more than one stage above their typical response (King and Kitchener, 1994).

Given that a combination of stage two and stage three reasoning is typical of the majority of high school students, it should be clear that reasoning at these stages is not consistent with the conception of reflective thinking embodied in CPI curricula, namely, that a reflective thinker is someone who is aware of a problem and able to bring critical judgment to bear on it. He or she understands that there is uncertainty about how a problem may best be solved, yet is able to offer a judgment about it that brings some closure. This type of judgment is based on criteria such as evaluation of evidence, consideration of expert opinion, and adequacy of argument. Most high school students are developmentally incapable of reasoning in this manner.

What are the consequences of attempting to teach students to think in a manner that they are incapable of? In addition to teachers failing to achieve their stated goals, it may also lead to student frustration and a loss of interest and motivation (Elkind, 1974; Ginsberg and Opper, 1988; Massialias, Sprague, and Hurst, 1975; Metz, 1978). Some researchers even found an inverse relationship between open climates in social studies classrooms and students' level of political efficacy (Braughman, 1975; Ehman, 1970; Long and Long, 1975; Zevin, 1983). The implication of these findings is that requiring youth to debate and/or solve intractable social and political problems where no easy solution exists may result in their actually becoming less knowledgeable and less committed to the values and processes of American democracy.

Data from classroom observations and interviews suggest that practical barriers may also exist in classrooms that feature discussion of controversial issues. In such classrooms, students often sense that the teacher is trying to do something to them and react negatively to teachers' attempts to make them into a certain type of moral person or citizen (D'Emidio-Caston and Brown, 1998; Leming and Silva, 2001). It has also been noted that some students wish to reserve the right to participate or not participate in discussions (Hess and Posselt, 2002). Pressure from the teacher and/or peers to participate is often seen as coercive. Only one form of activist citizen participation is legitimated in CPI classrooms and, if coerced to participate, students may resist (Hess and Posselt, 2002).[2]

Discussions in CPI classrooms also may tend to be dominated by verbally facile and interpersonally aggressive individuals. This elite looks down on those who can't defend their positions well. Those in the new lower caste develop hostility to the new elite (Hess and Posselt, 2002). Finally, students find that they can never come up with an unassailable defense for a position and eventually get frustrated with the process and retreat to trusted ideas and actions with which they are comfortable (Brookfield, 1994). This phenomenon, having to respond to repeated requests to examine and defend one's own reasoning, has been referred to as "roadrunning" since, like the cartoon character Wiley Coyote, just when a student thinks that he has developed a workable position on an issue, the boulder falls again.

This evidence suggests that a focus on controversial issues in the social studies classroom might have undesirable consequences, subverting the very objective it is designed to achieve. Some students may actually become less committed to the discussion of public policy issues.

AN ALTERNATIVE PERSPECTIVE

Is teaching thoughtfulness a hopeless task with school-aged youth? I think not, but the conception of what it means to teach students to think critically needs careful reexamination. In my judgment, the use of a curriculum focused on the solution of complex public policy issues to promote critical thought is inappropriate for school-aged youth. I propose three intermediate foci for public education that do not require of students forms of thinking beyond their abilities, yet contribute to their future capacity for reflective thought.

First, no U.S. history course is balanced or accurate without the study of the political and policy debates that shaped our nation's history. Students find these issues interesting and enjoy finding out about the players and the positions that each held in such debates. Learning about these issues can enhance students' enjoyment of history and government classes and result in increased learning. In the study of these historical and contemporary public issues, however, teachers should scale back their expectations and realize that what they see in their classes are not demonstrations of student irrationality or intellectual laziness, but rather expressions of a transitional rationality. Expecting students to demonstrate advanced thought patterns that adults have spent decades developing is unrealistic and counterproductive.

Second, social studies instruction should develop in students a rich and accurate store of information about our nation's history and institutions. This knowledge will provide the necessary basis for emerging reflective thought. To develop in students such a rich store of information in fields such as history and civics is not antithetical to the idea of teaching for thoughtfulness. Recent scholarship in cognitive science indicates that the major difference between novice and expert problem solvers lies not in the specific skills they possess, but rather in their stores of available, relevant, previously acquired knowledge (Hirsch, 2003). Skills are important but thinking critically is based on the knowledge one possesses.

This store of historical and civic knowledge alone has important consequences for the development of citizenship. Delli Carpini and Keeter (1997) and Milner (2002) contend that civic literacy is at the heart of education for democracy. Galston (2001, pp. 223-224) posits seven important links between civic knowledge and democratic citizenship:

- Civic knowledge helps citizens understand their interests as individuals and members of groups. The more knowledge we have, the better we can understand the impact of public policies on our interests and the more effectively we can promote our interests in the political process.
- Civic knowledge increases the ideological consistency of views across issues and time.
- Unless citizens possess a basic level of civic knowledge, it is difficult for them to understand political events or integrate new information into an existing framework.
- General civic knowledge can alter our views on specific public issues.
- The more knowledge citizens have of civic affairs, the less likely they are to experience a generalized mistrust of, or alienation from, civic life.

- Civic knowledge promotes support for democratic values.
- Civic knowledge promotes political participation (pp. 223-224).

While it may be debated whether traditional methods of teaching the subject matter of social studies will result in detectable changes in student thoughtfulness, it is clear that a rich store of information is an essential precursor to thoughtfulness and citizenship.

Third, the ability to resolve public issues is not the only aspect of critical thinking worth pursuing in schools. Beyer (1988) has conceptualized critical thinking as consisting of 10 abilities, listed here from simple to complex:

- Distinguishing between verifiable facts and value statements
- Distinguishing relevant from irrelevant observations or reasons
- Determining the factual accuracy of a statement
- Determining the credibility of a source
- Identifying ambiguous statements
- Identifying unstated assumptions
- Detecting bias
- Identifying logical fallacies
- Recognizing logical inconsistencies in a line of reasoning
- Determining the overall strength of an argument or conclusion.

Teaching to develop these abilities in the social studies classroom does not focus students on developing and defending positions on controversial issues. It does not embroil teacher and students in the developmental and phenomenological quagmires that often occur in CPI curricula.

CONCLUSION

Like the toy where the child hits one peg with a hammer only to have a different peg pop up, the progressive impulse to employ social studies to instill activism in youth and promote social change is a phenomenon that continues to "pop up" throughout 20th century education history. From the creation of social studies in 1916, to the Rugg textbooks in the 1930s, to the public issues emphasis of the 1960s and 70s, to the critical theorists and postmodernists of the 1980s and 90s, the "progressive" impulse has continued to mutate.

Over the past 20 years, postmodern thought and critical theory have supplied the framework for the work of the current generation of social studies leaders. In 1985, Nelson edited a special section on critical thinking for *Social Education*, the flagship journal of the National Council for the Social Studies (Nelson, 1985). His introduction, which has the typical critical perspective of what's wrong with America, states that:

> Critical thinking would be a primary pedagogical purpose . . . examining underlying structure and dominant cultural ideologies, would be expected. This would involve critical study of gender, race, nationalistic domination of social structures and knowledge. Thus content and method would be interrelated (p. 370).

In the critical theorists' view of social studies education, subject matter remains subordinated to the broader goal of radically transforming American politics and culture. One critical theorist (Alquist, 1990) expressed the role of teaching critical thinking thus: "This is not critical thinking for the sake of debate, argument or logical reasoning, but for constructive change, for the transformation of society" (p. 25).

With the focus on societal transformation so important to educational theorists, more basic questions in social studies education have not received the attention necessary to advance teacher practice.[3] The majority of social studies researchers ignore such knowledge-focused questions as what to teach, when to teach it, and how to teach it effectively. A review of the journal of the College and Faculty Assembly of the National Council of the Social Studies

(*Theory and Research in Social Education*) reveals a consistent neglect of research related to the identification of best practices. Of the 63 articles published in this journal between 1992 and 1997, none examined the influence of social studies curriculum on student acquisition of historical or civic knowledge (Leming, 1997).

While social studies theorists are aware that no research exists to support the idea of focusing the curriculum on the discussion of controversial issues, the idea will not go away. Five years after Parker's (1991) pessimistic observation regarding achieving thinking and decision making objectives in social studies—"the wish has remained so fervent, yet so unrealized" (p. 354)—Hahn (1996) noted that ". . . despite numerous calls for issues-centered social studies instruction over the years, the few schools that offered such programs have not reported their effectiveness" (p.25). More recently, Hess and Posselt (2002) noted ". . . that students can be taught how to discuss better is a claim supported by little empirical evidence—and virtually none in the recent social studies literature" (p. 284).

This persistent focus by the intellectual elite of the social studies profession on critical thinking and social change has led to the abandonment of the mission of teaching good quality content. As a result, we have a field without discernible progress in the craft and science of teaching. It has also left the field in disarray with researchers focused on issues that have little salience to students and teachers (Leming, 1989, 1992).

As we move through the new millennium, if social studies teaching is to improve, we must forego approaches that marginalize content and lack empirical evidence. It is time to focus on research-based curriculum development that will result in improvements in student understanding and appreciation of our cultural and political traditions. It is to be hoped that leaders of the social studies profession will stop attempting to use the discipline as a political tool to achieve ideological goals and instead begin to assume a responsible role in this important undertaking.

NOTES

1. Portions of this paper appeared earlier in (J.S. Leming, 1998).

2. The Hess and Posselt (2002) research indicates that it is in fact possible to teach students some of the skills necessary to participate in CPI discussions; however, they did not include comparison group data and their conclusions were based on changes in only three students.

3. Estimates are that less than 5 percent of secondary social studies classrooms utilize CPI instruction on a regular basis (Kahne, Rodriguez, Smith, and Thiede, 2000; Massialias et al., 1975; Newmann, 1991). This perspective on the goals of social studies education has remained primarily the province of academics and other educational theorists of a left-liberal persuasion

REFERENCES

Alquist, A. (1990). Critical pedagogy for social studies teachers. *Social Studies Review*, 29, 53-57.

Beyer, B. (1988). *Developing a thinking skills program*. Boston: Allyn and Bacon.

Braughman, J.E. (1975). *An investigation of the impact of civics on political attitudes of middle school students*. Unpublished doctoral dissertation; University of Maryland; College Park, MD.

Brookfield, S. (1994). Tales from the dark side: A phenomenography of adult critical reflection. *International Journal of Lifelong Education*, 13(3), 203-216.

Delli Carpini, M.X., and Keeter, S. (1997). *What Americans know about politics and why it matters*. New Haven: Yale University Press.

D'Emidio-Caston, M., and Brown, J.H. (1998). The other side of the story: Student narratives on the California drug, alcohol, and tobacco programs. *Evaluation Review*, 22(1), 95-117.

Dunn, A.W. (1916). *The social studies in secondary education: Report of the Committee on Social Studies of the Commission on the Reorganization of Secondary Education of the National Education Association.* Washington, DC.

Ehman, L.F. (1970). Normative discourse and attitude change in the social studies classroom. *The High School Journal,* 54, 76-83.

Elkind, D. (1974). *Children and adolescents.* London: Oxford University Press.

Galston, W.A. (2001). Political knowledge, political engagement, and civic education. *Annual Review of Political Science,* 4, 217-234.

Ginsberg, H.P., and Opper, S. (1988). *Piaget's Theory of Intellectual Development* (3rd ed.). Englewood Cliffs, NJ: Prentice Hall.

Hahn, C. (1996). Research on issues-centered social studies. In R.W. Evans and D.W. Saxe (Eds.), *Handbook on teaching social issues* (pp. 25-41). Washington, DC: National Council for the Social Studies.

Hess, D., and Posselt, J. (2002). How high school students experience and learn from the discussion of controversial issues. *Journal of Curriculum and Supervision,* 17(4), 283-314.

Hirsch, E.D. (2003). Not so grand a strategy. *Education Next,* 3(2), 68-72.

Hunt, M.P., and Metcalf, L.E. (1955). *Teaching high school social studies: Problems in reflective thinking and social understanding.* New York: Harper and Row.

Hunt, M.P., and Metcalf, L.E. (1968). *Teaching high school social studies: Problems in reflective thinking and social understanding* (2nd ed.). New York: Harper and Row.

Johnston, J., Anderman, E.M., Klenk, L., and Harris, D. (1994). *Improving civic discourse in the classroom.* Ann Arbor, MI: Institute for Social Research, University of Michigan.

Kahne, J., Rodriguez, M., Smith, B.A., and Thiede, K. (2000). Developing citizens for democracy? Assessing opportunities to learn in Chicago's social studies classrooms. *Theory and Research in Social Education*, 28, 318-330.

King, P.M., and Kitchener, K.S. (1994). *Developing reflective judgment: Understanding and promoting intellectual growth and critical thinking in adolescents and adults.* San Francisco, CA: Jossey-Bass Publishers.

Kitchener, K.S., and King, P.M. (1981). Reflective judgment: Concepts of justification and their relationship to age and education. *Journal of Applied Developmental Psychology*, 2, 89-116.

Kitchener, K. S., and King, P. M. (1985). *Reflective judgment scoring manual.* Denver, CO and Bowling Green, OH: University of Denver and Bowling Green State University.

Leming, J.S. (1989). The two cultures of social studies education. *Social Education*, 53, 404-408.

Leming, J.S. (1992). Ideological perspectives within the social studies profession: An empirical examination of the "two cultures" thesis. *Theory and Research in Social Education*, 22, 293 - 312.

Leming, J.S. (1997). Social studies research and the interests of children. *Theory and Research in Social Education*, 25(4), 500-505.

Leming, J.S. (1998). Some critical thoughts about teaching critical thinking. *The Social Studies*, 89(2), 61-66.

Leming, J.S., and Silva, D. Y. (2001). *Experiencing character education: Student and teacher voices*. Paper presented at the annual meeting of the American Educational Research Association, Seattle, WA.

Long, S., and Long, R. (1975). Controversy in the classroom: Student viewpoint and education outcome. *Teaching Political Science*, 2, 175-299.

Massialias, B.G., Sprague, N.E., and Hurst, J.B. (1975). *Social Issues through Inquiry*. Englewood Cliffs, NJ: Prentice Hall.

Metz, M.H. (1978). *Classrooms and corridors: The crisis of authority in desegregated schools*. Berkeley, CA: University of California Press.

Milner, H. (2002). *Civic literacy: How informed citizens make democracy work*. Hanover, NH: University Press of New England.

Nelson, J.L. (1985). The new criticism: Alternative views of social education (special section). *Social Education, 49*(5), 386-405.

Newmann, F.M. (1991). Promoting higher order thinking [Special issue]. *Theory and Research in Social Education, 19*(4).

Newmann, F.M. (1991b). Classroom thoughtfulness and students' higher order thinking: Common indicators and diverse social studies courses. *Theory and Research in Social Education, 19*, 410-433.

Oliver, D., and Shaver, J. (1966). *Teaching public issues in the high school*. Boston: Houghton Mifflin.

Onosko, J. (1991). Barriers to the promotion of higher order thinking. *Theory and Research in Social Education, 19*(4), 341-366.

Parker, W.C. (1991). Achieving thinking and decision making objectives in social studies. In J.P. Shaver (Ed.), *Handbook of research on social studies teaching and learning* (pp. 345-356). New York: Macmillan.

Threlkeld, A.L. (1931). *Character education: Tenth yearbook of the Department of Superintendence*. Washington, DC: Department of Superintendence of the National Education Association.

Winters, E. (1967). Man and his changing society: The textbooks of Harold Rugg. *History of Education Quarterly, 7*(4), 493-514.

Zevin, J. (1983). Future citizens: Children and politics. *Teaching Political Science, 10*, 119-126.

ABOUT THE EDITORS

Lucien Ellington is UC Foundation professor of education at the University of Tennessee at Chattanooga. Ellington is also co-director of the UTC Asia Program, founding editor of *Education About Asia*, and has authored three books on Japan, including *Education in the Japanese Lifecycle: Implications for the United States.*

James Leming is the Carl A. Gerstacker chair in education at Saginaw Valley State University. He is a former member of the board of directors of the National Council for the Social Studies and past president of the Social Science Education Consortium. He is also founding director of the Saginaw Valley State University Center on Economic Education.

Kathleen Porter is associate director of research at the Thomas B. Fordham Foundation and research fellow at the Hoover Institution. Previously, she worked as a fellow at the Progressive Policy Institute and most recently as a research analyst for the Council for Basic Education. She has taught social studies, science, and foreign language in middle and high school.

Selected Recent Publications

Publications are available electronically at our website, www.edexcellence.net. Single hard copies of most publications are available by calling 888-TBF-7474 or by emailing fordham@dunst.com. Additional copies are $10 each.

Charter School Authorizing: Are States Making the Grade? (June 2003)

This new report, released by the Thomas B. Fordham Institute, is the first significant study of the organizations that authorize charter schools. The report examines 23 states and the District of Columbia to determine how supportive they are of charter schools, how good a job their authorizers are doing, and how policy makers could strengthen their states' charter programs. Fifteen states earned grades of "B-" or better for their authorizers' work, but just four received similar marks for the policy environment in which charter schools and authorizers function. Massachusetts and Texas led the pack while California, Pennsylvania, and New Mexico brought up the rear.

Better Leaders for America's Schools: A Manifesto (May 2003)

This report, published jointly by the Fordham Institute and The Broad Foundation, contends that American public education faces a "crisis in leadership" that cannot be alleviated from traditional sources of school principals and superintendents. Its signers do not believe this crisis can be fixed by conventional strategies for preparing, certifying, and employing education leaders. Instead, they urge that first-rate leaders be sought outside the education field, earn salaries on par with their peers in other professions, and gain new authority over school staffing, operations, and budgets.

The Best of Both Worlds: Blending History and Geography in the K-12 Curriculum (February 2003)

Geography plays a crucial role in shaping history, and the study of history provides an important context for students learning geography, but K-12 teachers rarely take advantage of the complementary nature of these two subjects by teaching both in one integrated curriculum. This new report shows how the study of U.S. history can be enriched by blending geography into the curriculum. The centerpiece of the report is an innovative curriculum framework for studying the American past, a course in which each historical period is supplemented and enriched by the introduction of relevant geography.

Can Failing Schools be Fixed? (January 2003)

Will the sanctions for failing schools laid out in No Child Left Behind succeed in turning those schools around? In this new report, author Ronald C. Brady draws on the results of previous state and district efforts to overhaul failing schools to provide a glimpse at what may be expected from NCLB-style interventions. He finds that no intervention strategy has a success rate greater than 50 percent. Given that many interventions are unlikely to yield improved schools, he urges policymakers to consider additional options for children trapped in failing educational institutions.

The Approval Barrier to Suburban Charter Schools (September 2002)

Why haven't charter schools taken hold in suburban areas in most states? In this report, Pushpam Jain takes a close look at three states with high proportions of charter schools in the suburbs to see how they managed to introduce charter schools, and then compares them to one state with only a few charter schools to see what is blocking the spread of charters there. His conclusion: if a state sets up a system for authorizing charter schools where the only authorizing body doesn't want charter schools, there won't be many charter schools! (available at www.edexcellence.net only)

No Child Left Behind: What Will It Take? (February 2002)

Just one month after President Bush signed the No Child Left Behind Act into law, a provocative set of expert papers commissioned by the Thomas B. Fordham Foundation explore the legislation's key features: its testing and accountability provisions. The papers identify the questions left unresolved by Congress and the many hurdles facing the U.S. Education

Department and states, districts, and schools as they try to make this ambitious law a reality. The papers also offer suggestions for clearing those hurdles. (available at www.edexcellence.net only)

Making It Count: A Guide to High-Impact Education Philanthropy (September 2001)

Charitable giving in the U.S. is at an all-time high, as is the public's concern with the state of our K-12 education system. This guide provides practical advice for the philanthropist who is fed up with the status quo and eager to support effective education reform. *Making it Count* reviews the state of U.S. public education, examines different ways that philanthropists are trying to improve it, explains why some strategies work better than others, profiles a number of education philanthropists, and recounts the experiences of the Thomas B. Fordham Foundation.

Rethinking Special Education for a New Century (May 2001)

Recommending sweeping changes in federal special education policy, this volume of 14 papers scrutinizes the education now being received by 6 million U.S. children with disabilities. Jointly published with the Progressive Policy Institute, the report will help shape discussion of the next reauthorization of the Individuals with Disabilities Education Act (IDEA). It identifies the problems that now beset this important program, analyzes their causes, and suggests solutions. All who care about the education of children with special needs will want to read it for themselves. This publication is available for $10 per copy; visit www.edexcellence.net for ordering information.

Professionalism and the Public Good: A Brief History of Teacher Certification (January 2001)

Why does our system of teacher certification emphasize training in pedagogy rather than subject-matter knowledge? This report traces the emergence of state control over teacher certification. The focus is on efforts by the teacher education establishment to gain monopoly control over the licensing of teachers.

Whole Language Lives On: The Illusion of "Balanced" Reading (October 2000)

This report reveals that what's going on in many classrooms in the name of "balance" or "consensus" is that the worst practices of whole-language reading instruction persist, continuing to inflict boundless harm on young children who need to learn to read. How and why that is happening—and how and why such practices are misguided and harmful—are the subject of this report. (available at www.edexcellence.net only)

Good Science, Bad Science: Teaching Evolution in the States (September 2000)

More than one-third of the states get low grades for the standards they have developed for teaching evolution, according to this report. The report is the first comprehensive analysis of how each state handles evolution in its K-12 science standards.

Parochial Schools and Public Aid: Today's Catholic Schools (June 2000)

This report details how and to what extent public aid flows to church-affiliated schools. It finds that the amounts reaching parochial school students vary greatly from state to state.